Accelerated
Vocabulary

Strategies for Closing
the Achievement Gap
for All Students

Instruction

Nancy Akhavan

■ SCHOLASTIC

New York • Toronto • London • Auckland • Sydney
Mexico City • New Delhi • Hong Kong • Buenos Aires

For Jan Duke,
for loving words and opening children's minds to the power of language

Acknowledgments

This book grew from a few ideas discussed over coffee with a dear friend, and then bloomed into reality due to the generous support of a team of people. First of all, thank you to my husband, Mehran, and my daughters, Sayeh and Naseem, who are enthusiastic each time I sit down at the computer to write.

Thank you to the team at Clovis Unified School District in California for providing me with the opportunity to teach about language and literacy. These ideas and lessons have grown into strategies for teachers to help children find success in their literacy journey. I appreciate the caring consideration of all teachers in the Clovis Unified School District, and especially the teachers at Pinedale Elementary School, who gave me feedback about many of the vocabulary lessons.

I am especially grateful to Terry Cooper at Scholastic for her generous support of the idea of this book. Thank you to Ray Coutu, Jane Buchbinder, and Holly Grundon: I couldn't have dreamed of a better production team to work with. I am grateful to Gloria Pipkin for her care and nurturing of my voice when reading the manuscript. Most of all, thank you to my editor, Lois Bridges, who responds to my ideas and queries with verve and who shares her incredible gift of being present with me.

Cover design: Jorge J. Namerow
Cover photo: © Howard Grey/Photodisc
Interior design by Holly Grundon
Acquiring editor: Lois Bridges
Production editor: Jane Buchbinder
Copyeditor: Carol Ghiglieri
ISBN-13: 978-0-439-93037-6
ISBN-10: 0-439-93037-5
Copyright © 2007 by Nancy L. Akhavan

Table of Contents

CHAPTER 1

The Power of Word-Rich, Print-Rich Classrooms

Why the Time Has Come to Accelerate Student Vocabulary Development

This is a book about words:

- How to teach words

- How to teach the concepts connected to words

- How to foster a love of words and interesting, beautiful language

- How to expand student success through vocabulary

Make no mistake about it! This is a book about closing the achievement gap. Vocabulary is closely associated with intelligence and with knowledge (Nagy, 1988; Stahl & Nagy, 2006; Stahl, 1999). In fact, it is the foundation of success in school.

We don't have to teach this foundation as a prerequisite to connected, authentic literacy activities. Purposeful and effective vocabulary instruction should occur *in conjunction with* authentic reading, writing, and language activities that focus on increasing students' abilities to think, read well, and write. Vocabulary doesn't come first; instead, it develops *with* these indicators of success.

If the term *vocabulary instruction* conjures up ideas of boring lessons that you don't want to partake in, it is time to change your thinking.

Move your thinking away from:

- example lessons that involve preteaching lists of words

- children dutifully copying down definitions from the board

- children spending endless hours quietly looking up definitions from dictionaries

Move your thinking toward:

- connected word learning where the focus is on content units

- children brainstorming words they know and that are connected to a theme or content area

- example lessons that unveil how to think about words and how to remember word meanings

- explicit vocabulary lessons that teach new word concepts and meanings

- children learning new words from lots and lots of reading

- children discovering words and sharing them with the class

- having students become word sleuths, finding words they want to learn, or discussing new word meanings and use

Overall, your goal should be to focus on the wonder of words, on student engagement, and on the need to accelerate the rate at which children learn and know words. But before we launch into the *how* of teaching vocabulary, let's look at the *why*.

Why Accelerate Vocabulary Learning?

We cannot wait to teach children words. We are facing three important issues in education regarding vocabulary development:

1) A vocabulary gap exists among students in different socioeconomic groups.

2) Vocabulary knowledge affects long-term student achievement.

3) Vocabulary growth cumulates over time.

Our vocabularies include the number of words we know, information about many topics, and ideas and words within those topics. These aspects of word knowing directly affect our ability to read well, discuss ideas, write well, and understand academic conversations. Think of our vocabulary knowledge like this:

- Number of words we know (size)

- Topics and the words connected to the information (breadth)

- Ideas and words about the topics (depth)

Children need us to pay attention to their word learning; in short, a large vocabulary is correlated with reading comprehension and reading ability beyond third grade. The more words children know, the more they can comprehend what they read and, therefore, increase their knowledge. The reverse is true as well; the children who don't know many words tend to be children who don't read well, and the less they read and learn, the harder it is for them to catch up (Carlo, M. S., et al., 2004).

A Vocabulary Gap Exists

Recently I visited Susan Harper's diverse fifth-grade classroom in California's Central Valley. She has students who are learning English, students who receive resource services through special education, and students who attend enrichment classes because they have been identified as gifted. The day I visited Susan's class, her students were sitting around the classroom in groups, discussing the chapter books they had been reading. One group was reading *Hatchet* by Gary Paulson (2000); the students were deep in discussion about the main character. As one child would share, another child would jump in and elaborate. I heard snippets of conversation including "I disagree—let me tell you why" and "What were you thinking? It didn't happen that way in the book! Let me show you what page to read." Each child who spoke up enthusiastically stated his idea just before another student popped in a comment.

Another group was reading a different book, *Sideways Stories from Wayside School* by Louis Sachar (2004). This book happened to be at an easier reading level, and the interaction of the group was very different. In fact, there was little conversation happening at all.

"What are you reading?" I asked.

"Oh, this book the teacher gave me," Maria said as she waved the book in the air.

"Do you like it?"

"I dunno, I guess."

Not getting far with the conversation, I changed tactics. "Well, share with me what you have noticed so far about the book. What's happening?"

"The guy, he has a problem." Sarah answered, and then looked to her group members for support.

"Oh, I see." I said. I sat with the group a while longer and I was slowly able to help them pull their ideas about the book together. They didn't feel as comfortable as the first group talking about their reading and they were not able to discuss the character's actions. There was definitely a difference in the vocabulary usage between these two groups of students.

Large differences in the size of vocabularies exist among students. Betty Hart and Todd Risley (1995; 2003) conducted a long-term study measuring vocabulary growth in young children. They found that by the time children were 3 years old, the number of words they knew, and the types of language interactions they had with their parents, predicted later school success. By 3 years old, children from homes of professional parents had accumulated vocabularies of approximately 1,100 words, children from working-class families knew approximately 750 words, and children from homes receiving public assistance knew 520 words (Hart & Risley, 2003). Hart and Risley estimated the number of words children in different socioeconomic groups heard and compared the children's vocabulary size to that number (see Figure 1.1). The children of professional parents heard approximately 2,153 words per hour, children from working-class homes heard 1,251 words per hour, and children in homes receiving public assistance heard 616 words per hour. In addition to the fact that the poorest children had fewer words spoken to them, they heard more words spoken as declarative statements (like *stop* or *no*) and heard fewer descriptive phrases—such as explanatory responses to the unceasing *why* questions young children ask (Hart & Risley, 2003; Stahl & Nagy, 2006).

Estimated Number of Words Children Hear by Age 3

Socioeconomic status	Size of vocabulary at age 3	Number of words heard per hour
Professional	1,100	2,153
Working Class	750	1,251
Poverty	520	616

Figure 1.1   Source: Hart & Risley, 2003

Hart and Risley (1995; 2003) also looked at how this difference in vocabulary affected later school success. They found that the vocabulary knowledge of children at age 3 was indicative of their language skills at ages 9 and 10. These differences amount to a vocabulary and knowledge gap that affects children's ability to read, write, and develop knowledge.

Vocabulary Knowledge Affects Long-Term Achievement

The fact that there are differences among the vocabularies of young children points to one great reason to make vocabulary instruction *hot* in your classroom. Another reason is the long-term achievement of reading ability. The National Center on Educational Statistics reported that reading performance for students in the fourth and eighth grades who received free or reduced-price lunch was negatively associated with student achievement on the National Assessment of Educational Progress (NAEP) test (Livingston & Wirt, 2005). In other words, fourth- and eighth-grade students in homes receiving assistance did not perform as well on the NAEP test as students who did not live in poverty. Since reading comprehension is directly tied to the knowledge of words and word meanings, limited vocabulary skills in the primary grades and elementary school can adversely affect later achievement.

A special study by the U.S. Department of Education examined fourth-grade students' oral reading ability. Since vocabulary is tied to reading fluency, the results of this special study lead to some thought-provoking ideas about vocabulary instruction (Stahl, 1999). To read fluently, a reader must identify words quickly and easily, and fluent readers are able to decode and comprehend at the same time (Samuels, 2002). It follows that when children know more words, they are better readers (Hirsch, 2006; Stahl & Nagy, 2006).

One result published in this study of oral reading shows a relationship between fourth graders' ethnicity and their ability to read fluently. Students who read 130 words or more per minute were considered fluent readers. The study reveals a difference between white students, black students, and Hispanic students. Of the fourth-grade students considered to be fluent readers, 45 percent of them were white, 24 percent were Hispanic, and 18 percent were black. The level of poverty was negatively associated with student achievement. The study also revealed gender differences. Of these fluent readers, 44 percent were female and 33 percent were male (Daane, M. C., Campbell, J. R., Grigg, W. S., Goodman, M. J., & Oranje, A., 2005). Clearly, differences exist between minority students and white students. While the study did not make recommendations about vocabulary instruction, the study points to differences in the reading ability of children, and vocabulary size affects the ability to read well (Beck, McKeown, & Kucan, 2002; Stahl & Nagy, 2006; Stahl, 1999; Biemiller, 1999).

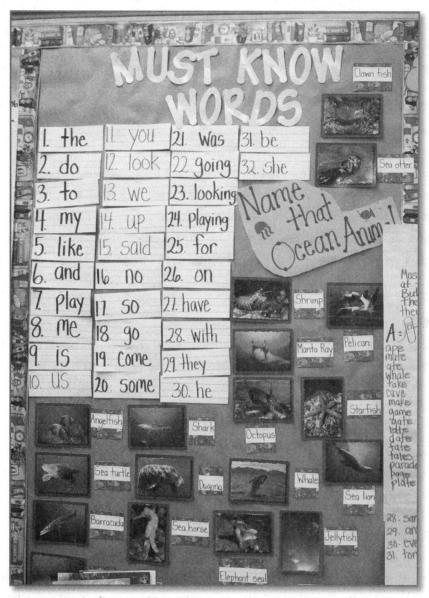

Figure 1.2: Word walls can combine content area words and sight words.

Vocabulary Growth Is Cumulative

A third reason that vocabulary instruction should take a priority in your classroom is because vocabulary knowledge is cumulative. The more words you know, the easier it is to learn more words. The more you focus on words and your students acquire language, the more knowledge and understanding of words they will accumulate (Shefelbine, 2004; Stahl & Nagy, 2006; Stahl, 2003). Word walls, as seen in Figure 1.2, help children learn words.

Children who know fewer words in the primary grades will not understand the vocabulary in the richer texts they encounter as they grow older. They will learn fewer words, and as they move into the upper grades, they will not be able to understand more difficult texts. Lack of exposure to a variety of words limits their access to more difficult texts and their exposure to a richer vocabulary. Therefore, children with smaller vocabularies will fall further and further behind unless we intervene (Neuman & Celano, 2006; Stahl, 1999).

While vocabulary growth is cumulative, it is also a slow growth process. Children can learn many new words a year, but they may not have a complete understanding of those words for some time. It takes repeated exposure to a word in many contexts for children to truly *know* a word. So by starting sooner, and exposing children to many words connected to content and information, we help them build large vocabularies. By focusing on vocabulary instruction with engaging, sustained activities, we can give children the learning necessary to close the vocabulary gap.

Vocabulary Matters

I am principal of a diverse kindergarten-through-sixth-grade school in California, and I work with my teachers to develop an outstanding literacy program that meets the needs of struggling readers, English learners, and gifted children. Actually, I feel that I run alongside my staff, learning from them every step of the way. Recently, we began to worry about the size of the children's vocabularies. The children were learning to read more proficiently, and we had more students reading at grade level by the end of third grade, but this achievement was not sustained in the upper grades.

In my work with teachers across the country as a staff developer and consultant, I have discovered the same trend. Children in second and third grade read aloud, or decode, well, but they have difficulty retelling and discussing what they have read. Teachers have also shared with me that their students in grades 4, 5, and 6 seem to slide, struggling to understand what they read, and struggling to write well. The growth of their vocabularies doesn't seem to keep up with the demands of content textbooks, rich nonfiction texts, and gorgeous literary children's chapter books.

Hearing and seeing this got me thinking about the fact that the students in my school and in schools I visited across the country struggle to acquire language. I thought about the ways in which I had taught vocabulary and how some of my best lessons (which I'd thought were great, although the kids were yawning) didn't focus students on acquiring word knowledge. Nor did the lessons I saw in other schools. I had tried to connect students to words with journals, and when this didn't work, I threw my hands in the air and resorted to the tried-but-not-true method of listing words on the board.

But copying words off the board wasn't getting me or the children anywhere. And some of the new strategies for teaching vocabulary, like having a vocabulary journal, felt more or less the same as copying words off the board. The journal was just a fancier way of doing things. I wasn't sure if the students at the school were acquiring many new words each year. I thought about it often and, as I worked with my faculty and others I met through my consulting work, I heard the same chorus repeated by caring, but frustrated, teachers: *It's a vocabulary problem.* If you are reading this book, I suspect you may have discovered the same issue in your classroom.

About This Book

This is a book for people who learn by giving an idea a run-through. I will share snippets of classroom scenes that helped me and the teachers with whom I work learn. These vignettes will lead to lessons that you can try immediately. This book is designed to help you improve your practice by *doing*.

I hope that by sharing these vignettes and lessons you will feel encouraged to give them a try. Each chapter is filled with teaching ideas. My desire is that some, if not all, of the lessons will work well for you and your students. Through the lessons and the modules of vocabulary instruction you will watch your students' vocabularies grow and deepen, and you will learn more about teaching vocabulary along the way.

This book begins by examining your vocabulary instruction over a year. You probably don't have many minutes in your teaching day for vocabulary instruction, as most of our teaching agendas are packed with curricular requirements and guidelines. This year of vocabulary instruction is designed to fit inside your existing structure. The only exception is adding 15–20 minutes a day for explicit vocabulary study. The other lessons will merge into your reading workshop, or reading block, your writing workshop, or writing block, your content study time, and your read-aloud time. The read-aloud time is one of the most important times of day for your students; this is especially so for upper-grade students whose vocabularies need to increase rapidly in order to keep up with the reading and writing they will have to do in middle school and high school. If you don't have a time set aside for read-aloud, you may want to consider making time in your daily schedule. When we read aloud, students acquire vocabulary through listening and thinking.

After planning several vocabulary units to carry your instruction through the year, this book will offer lessons for those units. The lessons will be organized around principles for vocabulary instruction, listed in Figure 1.3. These principles include:

- Creating a word-rich learning environment

- Making connections to words

- Engaging students with explicit instruction

- Accelerating vocabulary development through wide reading

Principles That Guide Vocabulary Instruction

Plan to Create a word-rich learning environment.

Plan to Teach concepts, not words.

Plan to Show children how to make connections between words.

Plan to Make your thinking transparent as a model for children.

Plan to Put content first and teach reading in fiction and nonfiction genres.

Plan to Engage children with intensive mini-lessons.

Plan to Mentor children during individual sustained reading.

Plan to Balance vocabulary instruction between explicit and implicit activities.

Plan to Spiral learning by using familiar methods and activities with new words.

Plan to Foster word learning by creating word-learning areas in your classroom.

Figure 1.3

About the Units

Planning curriculum for vocabulary instruction is very different from planning curriculum for reading or writing. That is because good vocabulary instruction should be tied to content. You might be thinking, "Well, then, why not just teach the words the teaching manuals list at the front of every chapter?" It's true that those words are there to help you organize, but as we explore the principles of effective vocabulary instruction, you will see that following a list is only one component of successful teaching.

The suggested units for a yearlong vocabulary study help you pay attention to words and to the rate at and extent to which your students acquire word meanings and make them their own. By creating a yearlong calendar you will be able to check your plans from time to time (each month, for example) and ensure that you are on track with your goals. Children need lots of exposure to many, many words and they need blocks of time to think about words, work with words, and connect words to information they are studying. The suggested units will help you create a classroom environment focused on the rigor of knowledge and the vocabulary acquisition that accompanies that knowledge.

About the Lessons

Great vocabulary instruction is multifaceted. That is what makes it difficult, but energizing and engaging at the same time. The lessons and activities in this book are only a few of the many types of vocabulary lessons that you can find in teaching books and manuals. The lessons and activities presented focus on the acceleration of vocabulary learning. Children learn best when what they are learning has relevance for them and when new information connects to information they already know.

These lessons aim to engage students in learning and to develop motivation. Motivated kids are kids who are learning word meanings and acquiring language. The ideas in the lessons focus on transferring new learning from short-term memory to long-term memory. I want my teaching—and your teaching—to stick. Many times I have taught a lesson or collaborated with a colleague aware that the new learning we were presenting seemed, for some children, to be flowing right through a sieve. These lessons are designed to help *all* children connect and engage with what we are teaching.

The lessons presented focus on children:

- learning something new

- engaging curiosity and concentration

- sustaining interest and finding utility to make a new word meaningful

- moving information from short-term memory to long-term memory

- connecting with words the way they connect with other media in their lives, including music, computer games, and reading information on the Worldwide Web

About the Assessments

Two issues hang like clouds over vocabulary instruction. We teach words, perhaps hundreds each year, and only a few words stick with the children. Which words stick we are never really sure without testing. These tests give only a small slice of the picture. We can't tell which words a child has stored in his receptive or expressive vocabularies. In other words, we aren't sure what words a child may truly know. By truly knowing a word, I mean being able to recognize it in print and/or aurally, and knowing the meaning in a split second. In order to prepare effective vocabulary lessons, we have to use qualitative assessments such as checklists, reading inventories, and anecdotal notes as well as tests.

These vocabulary issues are cause for worry. And worry we do. We worry so much that we turn to word lists to fill our lessons; we try preteaching vocabulary before a reading selection and we prepare vocabulary tests to see if students are learning. We scrutinize reading assessments, listening and watching for students to use content words, rare words, or big words in their conversations and writing. Vocabulary learning can seem invisible.

I believe that no matter how much we preteach vocabulary before reading or a content lesson, assign pages of dictionary definitions, have students fill reams of worksheets, and test to see if children have learned new words, until we help children connect to words in a meaningful way, they won't remember them. To remember a word is "recall," only one aspect of knowing a word. Our assessments need to inform our practice. We should use formative assessments to know and understand what our students have acquired. This book will provide ideas for assessment that have worked in classrooms and that give you a glimpse into your students' world of word acquisition.

The Power of Word-Rich, Print-Rich Classrooms

I have read in many different books and journals that the average child acquires between two to three thousand words per year. Overall research shows that school texts from grades 3 to 9 have approximately 88,500 distinct word families (Nagy & Anderson, 1984; Stahl & Nagy, 2006). That is a lot of words! That is more words than you or I can ever teach in an isolated, step-by-step process.

In an average fifth-grade classroom, some of the students may know thousands and thousands more words than other children in the room. Those children with the smaller vocabularies have smaller opportunities to learn and understand. The longer we wait to begin paying attention to the power of words, the further behind these children become. The situation is urgent.

Words don't jingle around inside of us like loose change but naturally attach to concepts and ideas we already know or learn. This is the power of a word-rich classroom: connections. You can connect children to the vocabulary size they need to be successful beyond elementary school; you can connect them to the much needed content knowledge that determines their reading comprehension abilities; and you can connect them to precise and beautiful language that enables them to write well. The time is now: Let's begin.

Important Points to Remember

Make Vocabulary **Hot** in Your Classroom

Vocabulary is closely associated with
intelligence and with knowledge.

Vocabulary influences reading comprehension.

Vocabulary growth is cumulative.

Children who begin school with a vocabulary
gap don't catch up without intervention.

Vocabulary Instruction Goals

Focus on a comprehensive approach to promote word learning.

Focus on long-term learning rather than on quick fixes.

Focus early on vocabulary development for young children.

Extend vocabulary development for older children.

Develop vocabulary for emergent and early fluent readers
as well as fluent readers in grades 4–6.

Focus on proven methods rather than the
tried-but-not-true methods of our past.

CHAPTER 2

A Year of Word Learning

Organizing Powerful Vocabulary Units

A Year of Word Study

A year of word study consists of five or six units of study (see Figure 2.1) dedicated to the processes and procedures of word learning. While our classroom atmospheres support word learning, to accelerate word learning we need to explicitly teach about words, not just teach words. The unit designed for the beginning of the year helps students settle into acknowledging words as vital and intriguing, and then the units move into explicit lessons to teach word meanings through word-learning strategies that include understanding definitions, word parts, and word use in context (Edwards, Font, Baumann, & Boland, 2004).

Four Ingredients to Student Learning

To help your unit development unfold smoothly, you want to ensure that students make connections to words and the concepts they represent; they need to make deep meaning from words and concepts connected to words (Scott & Nagy, 2004). When developing my yearlong curriculum, I build in time for conferring with other teachers along the way to ensure our teaching is on track. We check to see that our instruction is engaging students and integrating word-learning content and concepts. If we feel we are on track in the specificity of our instruction, then we look at our routines of assessment and reflection. We need to understand the data our assessments collect, and reflect on this information to tweak our lessons and activities to encourage powerful learning. Ideas for focusing on these four ingredients in student learning— engage, integrate, assess, and reflect—are summarized on the following pages.

Units of Study

Timeline	September	October	November	December January
Unit	Launching Word Learning	Power of Read-Alouds	Getting to the Power of Words	Going Deeper With Word Learning 1
Goals	Develop word awareness in your classroom and implement effective structures and routines to accelerate word learning.	Focus students on word-learning strategies. Students will become accustomed to the daily ritual and routines surrounding read-alouds.	Establish the routines, structures, and word-learning approaches that will become the bricks and mortar of your Fab Fifteen (15 focused minutes) time.	Provide intense instruction that probes the deep connections between ideas/words and content/reading and discussion.
Things to Think About	Develop vocabulary in three ways—through wide reading, specific lessons, and content studies.	Focus on the more difficult words that appear in children's picture books.	Focus on mini-lessons to teach vocabulary. Fifteen focused minutes each day makes a tremendous difference.	Each lesson presented in Getting to the Power of Words works for this unit as well. Choose academic words from your curriculum and pair with lessons to create a unit uniquely your own.

Figure 2.1

Units of Study

Timeline	January February	March	April	May
Unit	Learning Vocabulary in Content Studies	Going Deeper With Word Learning 2	Test Review	Going Deeper With Word Learning 3
Goals	Expose students to many words from content areas and foster word learning at three levels: receptive, associative, and generative.	Choose powerful lessons teaching words from read-alouds, nonfiction studies, and academic word lists, learn word strategies, and dig deeply into the meaning of academic vocabulary words.	Use local assessments to determine needed vocabulary review for standardized testing.	Continue with powerful lessons, choosing words that will carry children through independent summer reading and prepare them for the next grade.
Things to Think About	Choose content words with care. The bulk of direct instruction should be with academic words that span subject areas and genre. Words in content areas are powerful, but appear less often in children's reading and writing opportunities.	Create another lesson that meets the unique needs of your students. Returning to the methods and activities suggested in Getting to the Power of Words ensures that word learning is powerful and precise during the final months of your school year.	Review data from vocabulary tests from your school or district. Spend time reviewing test-taking strategies so that students can apply their word learning effectively to the testing genre.	Just because the end of the year is near, don't let up. Continue to challenge students with words and their connections to content, reading, and writing. End the year with a unit the combines explicit instruction with word-learning techniques to foster independent reading skills.

Figure 2.1

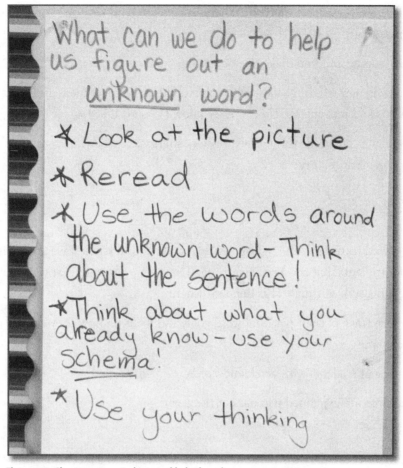

Figure 2.2: Charts engage students and help them learn new concepts.

Engage

We engage students through our classroom atmosphere and with precise, meaningful mini-lessons, when we:

- Share examples of beautiful, lyrical language

- Celebrate and accept students' favorite phrases and words

- Share a fascination with facts, ideas and information

- Share a fascination with words

- Act out word meanings

- Draw word meanings

- Honor students' attempts to discover and try new words

Engaging children in these ways motivates them to be excited about words, and enhances their learning, because it:

■ Focuses on helping children make deep meaning

■ Makes learning new words relevant by helping children connect ideas and words to other ideas and information they already know (Jensen, 1998)

■ Engages students' emotions through expression, sharing, role playing, signing, poetry, and content inquiry

Integrate

By integrating word learning with reading, writing, and content studies, we are paving connections for students that accelerate learning. Our memories work best when new information connects to schema. This happens when:

■ Students keep track of their personal word goals and focus on how they expand their vocabularies

■ Teachers present students with academic words

■ Word meanings are explained throughout the day

When we integrate vocabulary instruction, we make word learning a central part of our classroom community, and we do the following:

■ Focus on organizing word learning into patterns, as our brains seek connections

■ Focus word learning on concepts and not words

■ Teach students to infer word meanings from texts and create semantic maps for new word learning

■ Help students "see" words each and every day

Assess

Through assessment, we learn what students know and what they need to learn. Compare results from assessment to content standards and design units of study that meet students' needs and will accelerate learning. To do this:

- Listen to students read and focus on how they determine the meaning of unknown words

- Assess group knowledge of core words (Magic 8; see Chapter 5) and content words for a unit of study

To determine how our students are developing, we do the following:

- Develop an understanding of what they know about word usage

- Focus on teaching words they don't know, rather than reteaching something they already know

- Listen to them read to determine how well they infer word meaning

- Listen to them read to help them apply their word knowledge

- Assess their vocabulary knowledge appropriately, knowing that some words they are only acquainted with, and other words they own

Reflect

By reflecting on your instruction and student learning, you can align what you are teaching to what you planned to teach. Readjust plans to ensure that students are developing a broader vocabulary. Ask yourself:

- What words are evident in different writing genres, such as narrative, report writing, content writing, and writing about reading?

After instruction, we do the following:

- Reflect on student learning: Are students able to try new words?

- Reflect on children's word usage in writing, speaking, and academic conversation

- Ensure that our classroom atmosphere is a safety net for children to experiment and learn new words and concepts

- Focus on making our thinking transparent; model and make explicit learning and thinking that are implicit

Figure 2.3: Organize your library to capture student attention.

Classrooms That Support Word Learning

Space for words is important. We have space for furniture and equipment; we have space for books, backpacks, markers, and paper. We need space for words, too. If words are important, then finding places to organize and display words should take prominence in the architecture of your classroom (Blachowicz & Fisher, 2004) (see figure 2.2).

There are many ways to display words:

- Dedicate wall space to found words from poetry, books, and nonfiction.

- By using small but well-arranged areas to display words, not only can you get more on the walls, but you also make the words intriguing (see Figure 2.2). Create word work areas that display semantic maps, semantic feature charts, and content word banks (see Figures 2.4 and 2.5). Use *any* wall space instead of large bulletin boards.

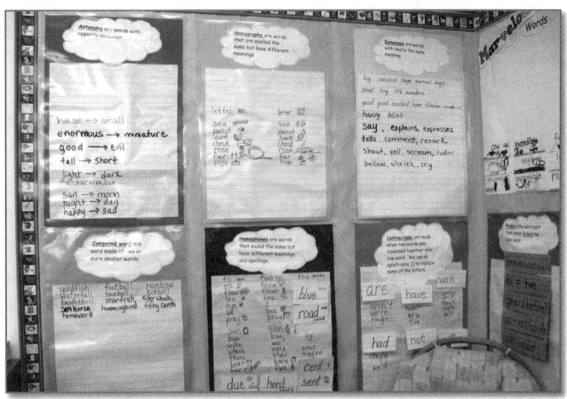

Figure 2.4: This word bank focusing on word structures is created by the teacher and the students.

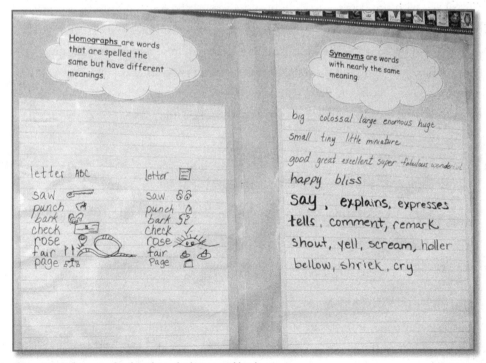

Figure 2.5: A close-up of a chart from the large word bank

- Drench your room in books. Don't put that book away after you read it! Display it in the classroom. The covers add print and interest to any small spot in your room. Make your classroom library a prominent place in your room.

- Flaunt words overhead. Hang word lists from the ceiling. You can use sentence strips linked together, strips of adding-machine tapes filled with words from a recent read-aloud or content lesson.

- Create word books and hang them on cup hooks in accessible places: near the classroom library, under the chalkboard, or in the class meeting area.

- Dedicate space to beautiful language and beautiful words (see Figure 2.6). Post "Beautiful Language or Beautiful Words" on a bulletin board, add a basket of sentence strips and markers close by and watch your children fill up the wall with words, phrases, and favorite sentences they find in their books, in school, and at home.

Sandwiching in Vocabulary Lessons

Word study needs to have shape and structure to be effective (McKeown & Beck, 2004). Even though your day is packed with standards, curriculum, and assessments, you can squeeze in a few minutes a day for word development. Fifteen minutes is fabulous. In 15 minutes you can change the amount of words a child has been exposed to, you can help some children *own* new words, and you can teach to language standards that perhaps your school or district requires (Beck et al., 2002). These fabulous 15 minutes easily fit inside daily schedules. The "Fab Fifteen" allows you to teach explicit vocabulary lessons and enables children to do all of the following:

- Acquire language for knowledge domains

- Connect ideas to words so that they can be learned

- Seek and provide information (making the lessons meaningful to students)

- Pay attention to words, word meanings, word parts, and word use

Consider the Words You Will Teach

If you think all your students need, in order to learn words, is a pencil and a piece of paper to write down the words you list on the board each Monday morning, think again. They need much more. You need to plan for word learning. *What words* are you going to teach? Some of the words you will teach because they are listed in bold print in your social studies or science books. Other words you will teach because they are useful, or elusive, or perhaps are words that connect ideas. Some words you will teach because they represent knowledge in a domain and will expand your students' understanding of information and the world.

Knowledge Base

Each child who enters your classroom brings with him his own unique knowledge base. It develops by experience, but much of that experience is developed through listening and reading (Hirsch, 2006; Nation, 2001; Pratt & Pratt, 2004; Scarcella, 2003). We expand our knowledge base when watching movies or TV. I prefer to dream that our children expand their knowledge base through wide reading of favorite subjects and novels. Tweens enjoy reading about other kids their age dealing with bullies, friendship, and first experiences in young relationships. They also enjoy exploring topics of interest in depth. The little ones in second grade revel in facts about dinosaurs, trains, and stories with common themes like the comfort of Mom's and Dad's arms.

These domains of knowledge present critical opportunities in terms of vocabulary instruction. Vocabulary development doesn't happen just by talking about words. It relies upon teachers connecting children to knowledge and information. As we've reached into the nooks and crannies of our daily schedules to find more time for language arts, we've whittled away the time we spend teaching science and social studies. This is a troublesome trend because these domains automatically support readers. Children who know a lot about the world read better; they draw on this knowledge to comprehend. The more text they comprehend, the more they connect with and enjoy reading, and the more they read, the greater their vocabularies become . . . and so the cycle goes.

Paying Attention to Students' Growing Knowledge Bases

Domain knowledge includes specific words and concepts associated with content areas. When preparing to teach a content study, you will choose vocabulary that mirrors the topic. The words you choose to focus on should concentrate on a concept and be connected to the theme of the unit. For example, in a civil rights unit the vocabulary might include: *racism, racist, freedom, bigotry, boycott, liberty, rights.* I might choose to introduce these words when teaching about Rosa Parks's grand move to stand up for civil rights by sitting down on a bus.

Connecting Books and Knowledge

The knowing and having of ideas is what keeps our classrooms ticking with wonder and intrigue. Children learn about the world, connect words to their new learning, and then connect concepts that they already understand to the new learning in order to own it. Much of this learning comes from books. While nonfiction, social studies, and science texts teach knowledge-base words explicitly, picture books often teach these words implicitly.

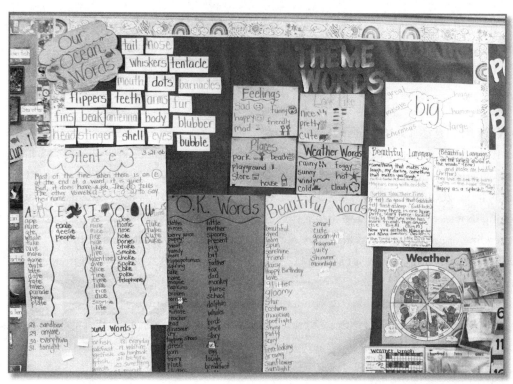

Figure 2.6: When the walls celebrate language, they become a reference tool for children.

To fully understand Fredrick Lipp's message in his book *The Caged Birds of Phnom Penh* (2001), children need to understand the concepts of poverty and oppression and hope. They also need to understand that the world is made up of different countries and each country has its own beliefs, traditions, and ways of life. These are rather big things to know and have in one's domain, or knowledge base. In *The Caged Birds of Phnom Penh*, Lipp lyrically describes a young girl's despair for her family. She wishes with great hope for her family to have a respite from hardship that includes a lack of food and fresh air.

On the other hand, *A Dinosaur Named Sue: The Find of the Century* by Fay Robinson (1999) teaches domain-specific vocabulary about the discovery of a large *T. rex* fossil. The domains enriched by reading this book not only include an understanding of a *T. rex*'s life, but also of paleontology and laws surrounding property rights.

About Useful Words

So what is the difference between words that develop in domain knowledge and useful words? Useful words are words that meet Beck, McKeown, and Kucan's (2002) Tier Two word category. Beck and colleagues described words as fitting into three categories, or tiers. The first tier of basic words rarely needs instruction: for example, *house, mother, sing*. Children develop an understanding of these words by exposure to conversation and reading. While we may teach these words as part of our reading program to help children access print, these are not words that we would focus on for accelerating children's vocabulary development. Of course, that is different for English learners, but even children learning English usually have a concept for Tier One words, and they need only to learn the label in their second language (Nation, 2001).

Tier Two words are those that appear frequently in reading, are part of a mature reader and writer's vocabulary, and are found across a variety of content areas and genres. These words tend to be conceptually difficult for an inexperienced reader or writer (Beck et al., 2002; 2003)—for example, *responsibility, curious, captain, virtuoso*. Tier Three words are connected to a specific domain of knowledge and appear infrequently in text. These words are best learned while studying a content area—for example: *cirrus, isotope, cumulus*.

Rather than uncover an academic word list on the Internet, or design one yourself, become acquainted with identifying Tier One, Tier Two, and Tier Three words. You would focus on Tier One words when teaching high-frequency words for reading fluency and comprehension. Your teaching spotlight would shine on Tier Three words during content study, and that leaves Tier Two words for your Fab Fifteen, where you are going to provide precise and fun instruction on the world of words.

Important Points to Remember

Criteria to Identify Tier Two Words

Importance and Utility:
Words that are characteristic of mature users and
appear frequently across a variety of domains.

Instructional Potential:
Words that can be worked with in a variety of ways so that students can build
rich representations of them and their connections to other words and concepts.

Conceptual Understanding:
Words for which students understand the general concept but which
provide precision and specificity in describing the concept.

Developed by Beck, McKeown, & Kucan (2002)

CHAPTER 3

Launching Word Learning

Creating a Robust Word-Learning Classroom

When you finish teaching this unit, you will have made a commitment to word learning in your classroom, and your kids will know it. Together you will have found words, discussed words, uncovered beautiful language, connected ideas to word definitions, dissected words, and sketched words to remember them. At the end of the unit, your students will have completed only tentative steps toward expanding their word consciousness, but they will continue to develop word-learning muscles through routine. Perhaps right now you feel primed to begin your forays into deeper word learning, but your students first need to develop "wakefulness" so that they can follow your lead. This launch unit will open the door for all of your students to notice and think about the words around them.

About the Unit

This unit is designed to be the first unit you teach during the school year. Through these lessons you will establish the routines, structures, and word-learning approaches that will become the bricks and mortar of your Fab Fifteen. (See Chapter 2.) Just as your reading workshop, spelling routines, and math routines are being established, your word-learning strategies will be created and reinforced.

This unit can last from two to four weeks and will stretch into subsequent units of study that streamline and organize words for explicit instruction. With this unit you'll teach the routines and procedures of word learning: precise lessons, vocabulary journals, semantic maps, word libraries, word collections, and fix-up strategies. Once your students develop familiarity with the strategies and routines, you'll quickly be able to get to the heart of vocabulary teaching: the words!

The unit consists of a number of lessons that expose children to the *how* of thinking about words and shows you *how* to accomplish this task in your classroom. See Figure 3.1 for the list of possible lessons that can occur in this unit. Of course, when you add your own flair, and design new structures and routines into your class by modifying the suggested lessons, you will make the unit your own.

Launching Word Learning

Lesson 1: Developing Word Awareness

Teaching Point: Knowing many words makes us better readers and writers.

Lesson 2: Using Known Words to Learn New Words

Teaching Point: We have to think hard to remember words we know and make connections to new words.

Lesson 3: Seeing Words in Our World

Teaching Point: Words create visual images in our minds.

Lesson 4: Discovering Wondrous Words

Teaching Point: Develop word consciousness by paying attention to words.

Lesson 5: Finding Beautiful Language

Teaching Point: Focus on how combining words enhances meaning and imagery.

Lesson 6: It's a Word Thing

Teaching Point: Quantity counts—brainstorming lots of words makes us aware of words and word resources.

Lesson 7: Picturing Words

Teaching Point: We write words from pictures in our minds.

Figure 3.1

The Essence of the Lessons

Teaching vocabulary is so important for students; for this reason, following a lesson sequence or process that has high impact for student learning is equally important. First, keep the lesson short. Think fifteen minutes, or fifteen fabulous minutes, otherwise referred to in this book as the Fab Fifteen.

■ First, get the children's attention . . .

I am surprised by the number of times I have worked with teachers who begin the lesson when some of the children aren't paying attention.

(I think this sometimes happens out of sheer exhaustion. I am no stranger to the classroom, and some days are more difficult than others.) Support yourself and your teaching by enticing attention rather than just demanding it. Entice children with rigor and with interesting subject matter. Entice children with success; no one wants to strive for something that feels like guaranteed failure.

■ Next, think "chunk" . . .

Our working memories have two shortcomings: capacity and time limits. A child's short-term processing capacity is very brief and requires immediate rehearsal to even begin to retain information. It is limited to about seven items that can be held in short-term memory before information is washed away (Wolfe, 2001). Chunking information together helps children remember, so short lessons that have a single focus with lots of opportunities for students to think or talk help them remember new information.

■ Then, think relevance . . .

Humdrum lessons that meet your state standards and fulfill a pacing plan won't guarantee children will learn. You have to make the words, terms, and concepts relevant for the students. When a lesson is relevant, it is contextualized, and more easily understandable to children (Cambourne, 2002). Then, the information makes sense and the action of sense making is a lubricant for learning. When children are engaged in relevant work, they are able to make deep, meaningful connections to words, with words, and between words. All of these are important to the acceleration of vocabulary acquisition. You don't want students to memorize facts; instead, you want them to connect to words and to rigorous, robust information about the world and about reading.

■ Finally, think pacing—quick, fast, lively, and interesting . . .

Well-paced lessons are mini-lessons with a single focus and chock-full of mnemonic devices such as real examples, visuals, pictures, drawings, discussion, and movement.

Making Words Relevant Even When, on the Surface, They Aren't

Children will disengage when they think something is only your idea. Choosing words that are disconnected from information they need, or that have little utility to them, will not engage students in word learning. Honestly, children are not that impressed if we think the vocabulary list is grand. I know this firsthand.

One summer my daughters, Naseem and Sayeh, thought it would be great to learn a word a day after they watched the movie *My Louisiana Sky* (based on the book by Kimberly Willis Holt, published by Hyperion, 2002). In this movie, the grandmother taught her granddaughter a new word when it related to something important that was happening in their lives. So, jumping upon my daughters' grand idea (I thought I had hit the mom jackpot!), I suggested that we look at the Word-A-Day Web site (www.wordsmith.org), and then discuss the word. Both of my daughters immediately shot the idea down. They wanted to learn the word in context, in discussion, not by looking up a word and "studying" it to remember. Children see things through a different lens than we do; however, they want to connect with us and receive our approval of their ideas. This is a delicate dance, and my daughters taught me to consider my students' wish for meaning. Children will engage, take risks, and work very hard to learn vocabulary when:

- The word/topic has utility to them (instead of to their teacher)

- The work is something they find interesting (instead of rote activities that seem to be time fillers)

- New language is meaningful (the words appear in books, lessons, experiments, and research we are expecting them to engage with)

Better Lesson Design Equals Appropriate Pacing

Designing an effective lesson isn't about what you write on paper, it is about what you do in action. Time and time again, I've worked alongside a teacher while she implements a mini-lesson in reading or writing, and time and time again we've looked at each other just as we sent the children off to work and said, "That was an '*And then . . .*' lesson (Akhavan, 2004). In an "And then . . ." lesson, I have taught too much, or overstepped the objective, forgetting to trust the children to understand my point. I realize that I've done this when I hear myself telling my students, "And then do this or that." This happens when we don't plan well; it happens to me when I don't keep my lesson-planning notes by my side during a mini-lesson, and it happens when I lose focus. Short mini-lessons that last only 10–15 minutes are a power punch for student learning. The lessons:

- **Claim attention.** "Okay, everyone, I've got some great words for us to pay attention to today. Some of you were wondering about . . . ."

- **Provide direct instruction** that teaches *one point*. "Brainstorm all of the words you know about the word in the middle of your map. These words connect to the main word in our memories."

- **Structure guided practice** that engages children with words. "Turn to your partner and tell him or her everything you remember about the word *isolated*."

In the lessons, these four parts are titled:

- *connect* (the part where you claim attention)

- *teach* (the direct instruction)

- *practice* (where you ensure structured, guided practice)

- *wrap-up* (reinforce the major teaching point)

1) Connect

By beginning with a connection, you are telling the students, "Listen up!—we are going to focus on learning" (Calkins, 2001). This "listen-up" phrase immediately focuses children's attention on the words they are going to learn. In a way, this preps their brains to receive new information and connect this information to things they already know. This should take about one minute.

2) Teach

Good vocabulary instruction is explicit (Beck et al., 2002; Biemiller, 1999; Stahl & Nagy, 2006; Stanovich, 1986). It tells children what they need to know, and it shows through modeling; however, it focuses on the *child's* role in constructing meaning. While the teaching in a mini-lesson is direct and explicit, it is not a lecture.

The teaching part of a mini-lesson avoids lecturing, which forces children to listen compliantly, as well as those last-minute pieces of information I call "And then . . ." segments. An effective mini-lesson also avoids the attempt to tap prior knowledge through questioning. Asking too many questions before we teach, or as a substitute for instruction, is a common occurrence brought about by our great desire to make sure children understand. When we too literally follow instructional methods that advise us to tap prior knowledge before a lesson, we often fall into a trap.

We've fallen into this trap when we teach through questioning and use ten minutes of a mini-lesson asking children about something they haven't yet been taught. Or, we question to remind children of what they have already learned. For example, "Who can tell me how to use the dictionary?" If students know what we are teaching, then we aren't focused on accelerating the children's vocabulary knowledge.

Teachers focus their Fab Fifteen by teaching words and concepts that the children don't know yet. Truly powerful teachers link this new learning to students' prior knowledge quickly and adeptly: "Remember last week when we retired powerless verbs in our classroom, those overused, nonspecific words that tell what someone or something is doing? Well, today we are going to brainstorm powerful verbs that we know. Verbs that have clarity, like saying, 'He rocketed across the floor' instead of saying, 'He ran quickly across the floor.'"

Using questioning as a strategy can be a powerful learning tool, but the focus should be on inquiry rather than on assessment during a lesson. Effective inquiry invites children to think about a word, wonder about its uses, purpose, and meaning. Inquiry does not assess a student's background knowledge, but instead provides a forum for delving deeper into the meaning and use of words, even when children are familiar with the words. Prior knowledge is best addressed in the connection part of the mini-lesson, in language such as "We have practiced using the dictionary, so today with a partner you are going to look up the definition of a word in your favorite book." It is important to tap prior knowledge when we want to wake up children's memory and grease the pathway for learning connections (Wolfe, 2001). But this can and should be quick and simple.

Children need to experience in order to learn and remember. The short-term storage in our brains for processing information is very short: about 18 seconds. Amazingly, this short interval functions well; we remember what has value to us, and our brains discard the rest—it's gone. Because of this 18-second holding pattern, it is important to engage children during the teaching part of the mini-lesson with visuals, discussion, ponderings, inquiry, connected examples, and emotion (Wolfe, 2001). When children interact with information, learning is enhanced and retained. Your lesson should be complemented by visuals or kinesthetic activities to help children hold on to information beyond the 18 seconds. That is why they need to engage with the new information. This should take about ten minutes.

3) Practice

After the first two steps of the mini-lesson, children need to engage in some type of conscious processing to solidify the learning process (Jensen, 2000; Wolfe, 2001). When children engage with information, they process it for themselves, so authentic, guided practice in a mini-lesson is quick, taking about five minutes. Obviously, you need to follow up during the day with independent time for children to explore words, try the new strategy, or seek words to share, but this five-minute practice can take place during your reading block (although in Chapter 4 you will see that the best activity for your reading block is *reading*) or as homework. You can also alternate your Fab Fifteen each day between lessons and guided practice: on Monday and Wednesday you teach a lesson, and on Tuesday and Thursday children spend the Fab Fifteen with independent or group activities. This plan leaves Fridays for assessment (see Figure 3.2). For a blank Unit of Study planning sheet, see the reproducible on page 137, in Appendix B.

4) Wrap-Up

While it will be tempting to spend more time than 15 minutes, it is important to wrap up the lesson and tell the children *when* they will be applying the new learning during the day. It might be during the reading block, an independent work time, or periods you set aside two to three times a week for group work. While vocabulary practice is important, lots and lots of time devoted to actual reading is more important. Children learn thousands of words a year through reading, and struggling readers need a great deal of time to read in school, as these are the children who usually don't choose to read after school. No matter how many words you can teach in 15 minutes a day, that explicit time will never match the time children spend reading. So, focus on the Fab Fifteen and designate lots of time for sustained independent reading.

Lessons for Launching Word Learning

Unit of Study   Name _____ Date _____

Monday	Tuesday	Wednesday	Thursday	Friday
Developing Word Awareness	We Know More Words Than We Realize	We Know More Words Than We Realize (continued)	Seeing Words in Our World	Seeing Words in Our World (continued)
Wondrous Words	Wondrous Words	Finding Beautiful Language	Finding Beautiful Language (continued)	Assess
It's a Word Thing	It's a Word Thing (continued)	Picturing Words	Picturing Words (continued)	Assess

Accelerated Vocabulary Instruction Scholastic Teaching Resources

137

Appendix B

Figure 3.2: Sample Unit of Study

Developing Word Awareness

Teaching Points

- Demonstrate that words are important to know and understand.

- Show how knowing many words makes us better readers and writers.

- Demonstrate how to make a word-definition card.

Prep Tips

- Prepare Words Are Important chart. See Figure 3.3.

- Have a blank index card prepared like the one pictured here (a reproducible is on page 152, Appendix B) to create large word cards.

- Index cards can be stored in a file box; the large version can be stored in a folder.

- Have the students save cards to create their own personal dictionaries.

Word Card	Name _____ Date _____
Word	**Definition in my own words.**

Connect

"Words are important to me, and you'll understand soon how important they are to you. Because we feel this way, we are going to spend time this school year focusing on words and the connections between words and our reading. I want you to expand the number of words you know."

Teach

"Words are important; they help us read better, communicate, and understand information. Look at the important ideas I wrote on the chart." Point to Figure 3.3. "We are going to explore important and favorite words in our classroom. I have a lot of favorite words, but I am only going to share one of them with you today. This word is *oscillate*. I like this word because of how it sounds to me and how it feels in my mouth when I say it. *Oscillate*. I am going to write the word on this card." Write in front of the class to model how you want them to write their words. "I am writing the word on the left side of the card. Make sure you leave the other part of the card blank."

"*Oscillate* means to move backward and forward. It actually has more than one meaning; the other meaning of *oscillate* is to be indecisive. So . . . when your best friend can't make up his mind about the type of ice cream he wants to eat, he *oscillates* between chocolate and vanilla. I am going to write the definition down in my own words on the right side of the card."

"In a minute you are going to make a word card just like this with a partner. We are going to add the word cards to this chart I have on word learning. Let's review the chart so you know what is important about words in our classroom." (See Figure 3.3 for an example.) After the word cards are completed, hang them on the sides or along the bottom of the chart.

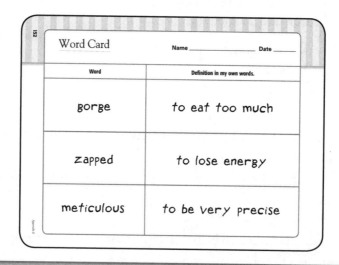

Words Are Important in Room 17

Knowing many words helps us read better.

Knowing many words makes our writing better.

When reading, if I don't know a word I can ask a friend, think about how the word is used and assume what it might mean, or I can use a dictionary.

When writing, I should choose powerful words instead of weak words.

152

Word Card	Name _____ Date _____
Word	Definition in my own words.
gorge	to eat too much
zapped	to lose energy
meticulous	to be very precise

Figure 3.3: Record important ideas during lessons on charts to make lessons visual.

"Since it is important for us to know many words, let's brainstorm some of the words we know and I will write them on the chart." Make sure to accept all the words any student thinks of, no matter how small. The point is to get their thinking muscles working. Write the words on a blank piece of chart paper. "Now that we've brainstormed a lot of words, we are going to make a word card just like I did." Show card again.

Practice

"I want you to think of a word that you really like. Maybe you like how it sounds or what it means. When you have a word in your mind, give me a thumbs up." For management purposes I pair up students so they can help one another to think and respond. Before beginning the rest of the mini-lesson, I have students sit next to a partner. "Tell your partner your word, and tell him or her what you think it means."

Give students time to share. Hand out a card and a marker. Have partners choose a word to write down. Then have the children write the definition in their own words. Figure 3.4 is an example of the word card for *oscillate*.

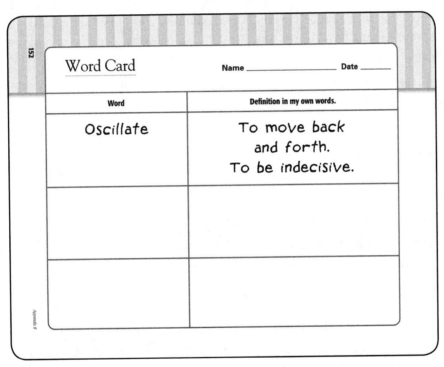

Figure 3.4: Children write their own definition of the word to make connections to the word's meaning.

Wrap-Up

"We listed many words that we know today, and I went over a few reasons why words are important to me. Now I want you to share your word with two other partner groups. When you are done, come up and add the card to the chart."

LESSON 2

Using Known Words to Learn New Words

Teaching Points

- Develop word awareness with students.

- Demonstrate to children that they know a lot of words already and that they need to think to retrieve the words from memory.

- This lesson provides an informal assessment opportunity. Notice which students brainstorm a lot of words; these are probably the students who read a lot. In future lessons, pair these students who seem to have a large generative vocabulary with students who have smaller vocabularies.

Prep Tips

- Create chart heading (such as Words That Begin With L; see page 39).

- Have small sticky notes for each student.

Connect

"Yesterday we brainstormed words we know and enjoy. We also shared those words with one another. Today we are going to brainstorm words again, but instead of thinking of words we enjoy, we are going to think of as many words as we can in a short time."

Teach

"We are going to have a bit of fun today brainstorming words that start with the first letter of our school's name. So, since we are Pinedale Elementary School, we are going to brainstorm words that start with P." You should use the first initial of your school, or the initial of your last name, or of your school mascot. Any initial that has some connection to your classroom works well. "I want you to spend one minute alone to think of as many words as you can. Then you will work with a partner for about five minutes. When I think of one word, at first it is hard for me to think of other words. It is like my brain feels slow. But when I wait and think a bit, all of a sudden I remember more words. So, you have to relax when you get stuck and let the words come to you."

Practice

Next show students the chart. Figure 3.5 on page 39 is an example of what the chart should look like when filled out. The photo below the chart (Figure 3.6) shows examples of student thinking. Tell the students, "I am going to give you a few sticky notes and I want you to write the words you

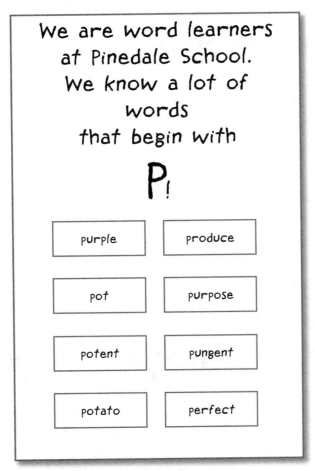

We are word learners
at Pinedale School.
We know a lot of
words
that begin with

P!

purple	produce
pot	purpose
potent	pungent
potato	perfect

Figure 3.5: Boosting creativity letter by letter

think of. After one minute I am going to have you work with your partner." Pair the students up and hand out the sticky notes. Repeat the directions about working on their own first, and tell them you will give a signal when it's time to work with their partner.

Wrap-Up

Have students post their words and then read the words out loud so all students can hear them.

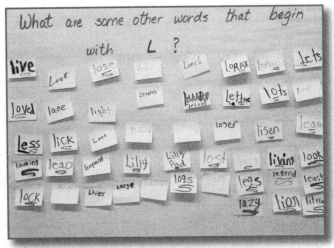

Figure 3.6: Children brainstormed different words that begin with *L*.

Seeing Words in Our World

Teaching Points

- Words create visual images in our minds.

- Words connect to other ideas, images, and information we already know.

Prep Tips

- Read *Long Night Moon* by Cynthia Rylant (2004) prior to teaching the lesson.

- Prepare chart for word descriptions. See Figure 3.7 below.

- After the lesson, display student-made charts so that the lesson goes beyond the discussion of words to actually seeing the words.

Month	Name of moon	Descriptive words
January	Stormy moon	Clouds, rain, dark, lightning, thunder, mist, ice, sleet

Figure 3.7: Descriptive words from *Long Night Moon* by Cynthia Rylant (2004)

Connect

"For the last two days we have brainstormed words we know and have come up with many interesting words. Now we are going to think about words in a book and how they make us think of other words."

Teach

"Cynthia Rylant's writing in *Long Night Moon* is very descriptive; many of the phrases make me see other images that I can describe in words that come to my mind. I see words in my mind because of Cynthia Rylant's writing. Let's look at how she describes the moons in this book." Show students the chart in Figure 3.7. "The first moon is the January moon. She calls this moon the *stormy moon*. When you hear the phrase *stormy moon*, what other words pop into your mind?" List the words that the children think of on the chart. "When we thought of the word *stormy*, we thought of many words to describe *stormy*. This is really important because good readers and good word wizards connect words in their head to learn them." Reinforce what good word learners do by repeating this phrase.

Practice

There are eleven more moons to describe from the book. Split your class into eleven groups; give each group the name of one moon. Have them describe the word that Cynthia Rylant uses to label the moons in her book. Have the groups brainstorm other words and write the words on a small chart to hang on the wall.

Wrap-Up

Have each group share their small chart with the class. To make this go quickly, have the groups share only a word or two. Display the charts in the room.

To extend this lesson, repeat it several times during the launch unit with any book that describes objects with interesting language. (See Lesson 7 for another "picturing" word lesson.)

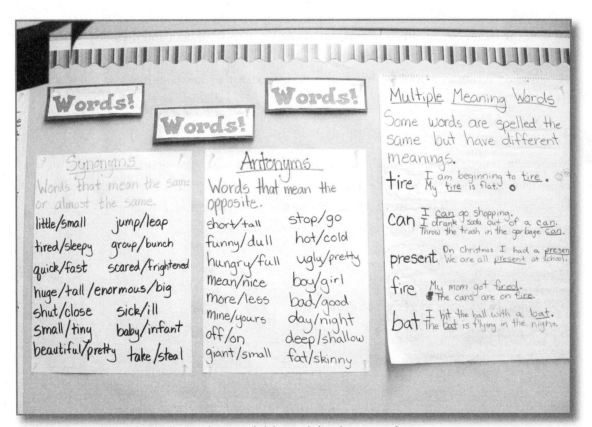

Displaying the words your class brainstorms increases their interest in learning new words.

Discovering Wondrous Words

Teaching Points

- Develop word consciousness.

- Encourage students to find words in their world outside of school and share them with the class.

Prep Tips

- Prepare a bulletin board or wall area labeled "Wondrous Words."

- Prepare a basket of sentence strips and markers and place it by the Wondrous Words display to encourage students to post their words independently.

Connect

Kick off the lesson by explaining to children what wondrous words are, and then display them in the classroom. Wondrous or marvelous words are favorite words—the words you save in the back of your mind because you love the way they sound, or what they mean, or how you feel when you say them.

Teach

Recognizing wondrous words and discussing the words, making them important in your classroom, is an ongoing way to celebrate words with your students throughout the year. This lesson points out words that are important because of utility, sound, beauty, or message. The instruction is focused on finding and discussing words that are:

- Rich

- Representative of new contexts

- Fascinating

- Enthralling

When teaching this lesson make sure to describe to children the meanings of new words that you find marvelous or wondrous. Explain your thinking and encourage the children to find words they really like in their books at home, in the neighborhood, or in other places and bring them in to

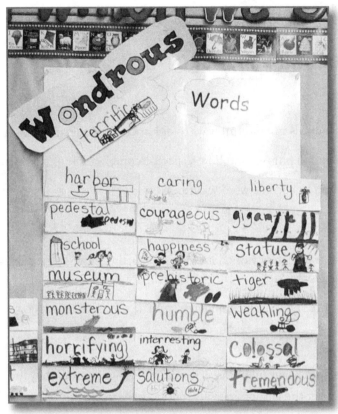

Figure 3.8: Third-grade teacher Laurie Cruz encouraged children to bring wondrous and marvelous words to school each day.

post on the board. Students can be responsible for writing the words on cards and posting them by themselves. It helps to have a basket filled with word-learning tools like index cards, thin and thick markers, tape, and sentence strips in a location near the Wondrous Words board. This encourages the children to post words without having to dig up the supplies from elsewhere in the room.

Laurie Cruz, a third-grade teacher in California, celebrates both wondrous and marvelous words in her classroom (see Figure 3.8). She writes the words the children find on the cards, and then the children illustrate the cards with their image of the word's meaning. By using nonlinguistic representations like drawings, Laurie helps her students remember the new words' meanings. In their research, Robert Marzano, Debra Pickering, and Jane Pollack (2001) found a strong correlation between nonlinguistic representations and learning. When children draw word meanings, they remember the words and provide visuals for the other children to connect with.

Wrap-Up

Since this lesson launches the children to find words outside of class time, there is no direct practice. Remind the children that their homework that night is to bring in words, write them on the cards, explain their findings to the class, and post the words in the designated area.

LESSON 5

Finding Beautiful Language

Teaching Points

■ Authors combine words in powerful ways to enhance meaning and imagery.

■ Focus on the beauty of phrases and how a specific combination of words can be powerful.

■ Encourage children to become word wizards.

Prep Tips

■ Prepare overhead transparency or chart with the poem "Snow Toward Evening" by Melville Cane, 1994. (See Figure 3.9.)

■ Prepare chart. Write "Descriptive Language" on the top of chart paper. (See Figure 3.10.)

Connect

When children recognize beautiful phrases, words, and language use, they are beginning to read and ponder not just what the author is saying, but how the author is saying it. They are becoming word wizards!

Children often take for granted the way something is written and rarely stop to ponder why or how an author decided to use certain words or arrange them in a certain powerful way. As children find and discuss beautiful language, celebrate it in your classroom. Finding descriptive language and adding it to the walls in your room is a way for children to personalize the print in your classroom. Sometimes they might choose funny phrases, pretty-sounding phrases, or phrases that create powerful mental images. All of these are important, and most often include a rare word or two. Rare words are words that appear less often per one thousand words in most texts (Stahl & Nagy, 2006). While we don't want to overwhelm children with exposing them to too many rare words at once, a new word mixed in with other words children know is an explicit way to expose children to new words in easy and nonthreatening ways.

"We've been looking at lots of words during the last few weeks to dig into vocabulary. But looking at words goes beyond looking at individual words; we need to see the phrases they connect to and see how powerful these phrases are."

Teach

"When I'm reading, sometimes I come across phrases I think are so powerful and beautiful that they take my breath away. We are going to consider the phrases in a poem today, and then we are going to look at other poems and books and see if there are phrases that catch our eye." Read the poem to the class.

"My favorite phrase in this poem is *millions of petals cool and white.* I am going to write this phrase on this chart that I labeled 'Descriptive Language.' When I read this, I see petals floating in the air, but I also know that the petals the author refers to are snowflakes." Ask the class to share any other phrases they like from the poem and add these to the chart.

Practice

Set out picture books and poetry books. Have students browse for a few minutes and see if they can find any phrases to add to the chart. They may not recognize what they think of as beautiful right away because they won't want to make a mistake. Continue to model, model, and model and tell them that the beauty of the phrase is in the eye of the beholder. See Figure 3.10 for an example of a descriptive language chart for a different book, *My Rotten Redheaded Older Brother* by Patricia Polacco (1998). This example shows how the children began to think about language and what they asked the teacher to record.

Wrap-Up

"I think poems are filled to the brim with descriptive phrases, so if you find anything to add to our chart, let me know and I will write it down."

Snow Toward Evening

Suddenly the sky turned gray,
The day,
Which had been bitter and chill,
Grew soft and still.
Quietly
From some invisible blossoming tree
Millions of petals cool and white
Drifted and blew,
Lifted and flew.
Fell with the falling night.

Figure 3.9: Poem "Snow Toward Evening" (Cane, 1994)

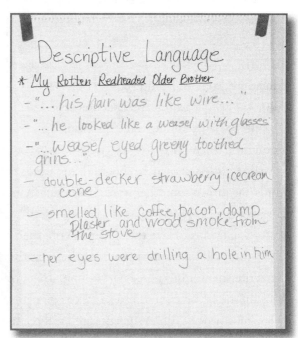

Figure 3.10: Descriptive Language chart for *My Rotten Redheaded Older Brother*

Creating "It's a Word Thing"

Teaching Points

- Have fun with words and focus on generative word use.

- Brainstorming lots of words makes us aware of words and word resources.

- Generative word use encourages children to *generate* words from memory and use them effectively orally and in writing.

Prep Tip

- Create several small posters using the reproducible on page 154 (legal-size paper works well), or hand-write "It's a Word Thing!" on construction paper. Replace the word "Word" with an alphabet letter. Your charts would read, "It's a B thing," etc.

Brainstorm words below the line that begin with the letter in the box.

Name _____ Date _____

It's a Word Thing!

Write a letter in the box.

Teach

Sometimes you need a fun activity that promotes word learning and encourages students to delve into resource materials around the room. This activity gives some flavor to the lesson by throwing in a bit of competition as well. This lesson is more about finding words from different resources than about learning the words' meanings—in other words, the focus in on quantity, not quality.

Break the class into teams of four or five students and assign them a letter. Give them the poster you created. Have the students write their letter in the blank space or box on their poster. The teams will list as many words as they can think of that begin with their letter. The children can write the words on the chart or hang them off the chart using strips of paper. You can spice up the lesson by initiating a bit of competition among the groups to see who can think of the most words. When students are finished, hang the word charts around the room for an instantaneously word-filled environment. Resources for finding words include children's memories, the classroom walls, textbooks, picture books, novels, resource materials, thesauruses, and dictionaries.

LESSON 7

Picturing Words

Teaching Point

- By focusing on the pictures children have in their minds, they can connect words to other ideas and develop a better understanding of a word's meaning.

Prep Tips

- Make photocopies of the Word Picture Activity (page 151 in Appendix B).

- Make a larger version of the Word Picture Activity on a chart.

- Create a short list of target words from current academic units.

Connect

"Today we are going to describe the mental images that pop into our minds when we hear a word. By focusing on what we see in our minds, we can hook words together to learn more words. We can also help one another learn new terms for images, ideas, and feelings."

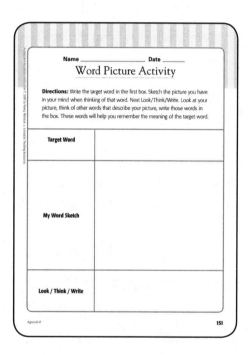

Teach

Anastasia Suen is a children's author who has written a book on writing and teaching writing titled *Picture Writing* (2002). Her book provides a great approach for getting children to write words and become word-aware.

Suen suggests an approach in which a writer pays attention to the pictures in his or her mind and writes from these pictures. Children can do this to connect words to schema, memories, and new learning. This activity helps children become word-aware and grasp descriptive language. When children describe a picture in their minds, they are working with words that are "just right" in terms of their present learning level, though of course we want to nudge children to use new words as well.

In Picturing Words, children can use a thesaurus, or the classroom's word walls, to try a new word or two in their descriptive lists. Children will be trying out these new words by connecting them to meaningful memories or thoughts. Tying new words to known concepts helps children remember and gives them a safe way to try a new word out without feeling embarrassed. If the word doesn't work because the definition is off, they can erase it.

Begin the lesson by choosing a few target words. Have these words prepared and handy. Use the chart you created to guide a think-aloud process that reveals your thinking when you picture a target word in your mind. Discuss with children what you are thinking while you write the words and sketch your picture on the chart. The steps to the process are as follows:

- Start with a target word.

- Next, sketch out what the word means.

- Then, write other words that describe the target word.

- If appropriate, have a few children look up the target word in the thesaurus and add synonyms to the Look/Think/Write box.

Wrap-Up

Students can use a Word Picture Activity sheet when reading independently, learning core words, or keeping track of words assigned in class.

Important Points to Remember

The 18-Second Holding Pattern

According to Wolfe (2001), the brain has a short-term storage capacity for processing information.

This capacity is 18 seconds.
Capitalize on the 18-second holding pattern
by reinforcing what children need to remember during your mini-lesson:

Focus on one major point.

Think rather than be passive.

Use visuals, repetition, discussion, and connected examples.

The Design of Effective Mini-Lessons

Connect

(Wake Up the Brain)
lasts about one minute

Teach

(Explicit Instruction)
lasts about ten minutes

Practice

(Guided and Authentic)
lasts about five minutes

Wrap-Up

(Transition)
a sentence or two highlighting learning

CHAPTER 4

Read-Aloud Lessons

Using Picture Books to Broaden Students' Vocabularies

W ords can make all the difference in the world. If left on their own, most students will skim over the words they don't know in a text and not stop to wonder what a word might mean. We teach our children to skip over words they don't know as a reading strategy to help them begin their first foray into the world of books; it is a strategy that works. But there comes a time when children need help to learn and appreciate word meanings. By choosing a time of day to focus on vocabulary, we are stopping to appreciate those words and model for our students how to infer word meanings, and more important, understand the power of precise and rich language.

For children who are becoming fluent readers and moving into texts with more print on the page, one hundred becomes a magic number. One hundred words is the number I often use to assess a student's ability to read. I mark off one hundred words, listen to the child read, and then calculate the miscues. One hundred words do make a difference for the children who understand them: they are able to access text rapidly and with comprehension. One hundred words also make a difference for children who don't understand all of them, or the combined meaning that arises from the text: they become frustrated and read less.

Gather your favorite books around you and glance at the first 100 words. What do you notice? What about the next 100 words? If you have gathered your favorite chapter books around you, open one to an exciting part of the book. What type of language does the author use? What would a child miss if he didn't understand the vocabulary?

Sometimes we take for granted that children understand what we are reading to them. The first 100 words in *A Grand Old Tree*, a beautiful picture book (see Figure 4.2) by Mary Newell DePalma (2005) seem simple enough, but if a child doesn't understand what squirrels do, or the life cycle of plants, she might miss the message this beautiful book offers. The first 27 words (see Figure 4.1) prepare the reader to understand the importance of the tree.

> Once there was a grand old tree.
> Her roots sank deep into the earth, her arms reached high into the sky.
> She was home to many creatures.

Figure 4.1: Words from *A Grand Old Tree*

Figure 4.2: Front cover of the book *A Grand Old Tree*

The words in Mary DePalma's writing sing and gently carry the reader through the grand old tree's life, but they also do something else which, as seasoned readers, we may take for granted: The words introduce concepts and ideas—*sank, nestled, scurried, bore, sowed, basked,* and *swayed.* These are words that children might gloss over if they don't understand them. Also, consider these 52 words (Figure 4.3) from the article "Cool Inventions" in *National Geographic Kids* magazine (2006).

> "Ever wish you could ride your bike on water? With the pump-bike, you can! Instead of pedaling, you bounce. And instead of doing wheelies down the sidewalk, you skim smoothly along the surface of the water. Using the handlebars to steer, you propel the bike forward by bouncing up and down . . ."

Figure 4.3: Words from "Cool Inventions"

Or consider these 60 words containing descriptive phrases (Figure 4.4) taken from the first few pages of *Blue Jasmine* by Kashmira Sheth (2004).

Only a few months earlier, when the mango trees were jeweled with purplish-green leaves and milky-white blossoms, a letter came that changed everything . . . . Pappa was a microbiologist. He loved his work, and some days when he got busy doing experiments in his laboratory, he forgot to eat lunch. On these days my grandmother made one of his favorite dishes for dinner.

Figure 4.4: Descriptive phrases from *Blue Jasmine*

Just imagine how deep children's understanding of the plight of the young heroine, Seema, would be if they perceive how she sees the world around her: with jeweled mango trees and a hard-working microbiologist as a father. Just imagine how lost the reader might be who doesn't grasp the meaning of these same words and phrases: *jeweled with purplish-green leaves, milky-white blossoms, microbiologist, experiments in his laboratory*, and *dishes for dinner*.

Beginning the Unit of Study and Read-Aloud Time

This is a unit of study for October. It is the second vocabulary unit to teach, following the unit that launches word study. The unit is designed to acquaint children with the different ways you will teach vocabulary through read-alouds during the year. This unit is designed to be taught over two or three weeks. By concentrating on read-alouds and the ways to learn vocabulary from the read-alouds, the children will become accustomed to the daily ritual and routines. This way, as the year develops, you can get to the teaching more quickly because the children will be familiar with the different activities that take place during and after reading.

When we teach vocabulary well, we develop a culture of inquiry. Developing an inquiry stance allows us to push children to discover learning for themselves and make their own connections to information and words rather than borrow ours; we enable them to learn information that expands their worlds. That is what vocabulary instruction is about—learning information—and information is power.

Pick a time of day for your read-aloud. Make it a priority so that you don't accidentally skip over it. In other words, waiting until the 15 minutes before recess begins is a recipe for missing many read-aloud moments when other subjects run overtime. Gather students on the floor, or create a meeting area where children can concentrate on the read-aloud and appreciate it for the importance that it will take on in your curriculum. I have found that students in grades 4, 5, and 6 enjoy hanging out on the floor *away* from their desks.

Read-Alouds Complement Sustained Independent Reading

Stahl and Nagy (2006) state, ". . . wide reading is the single most powerful factor in vocabulary growth" (page 49). I agree with this statement; however, you cannot just tell children, "go off and read" and expect their vocabularies to spontaneously grow. Not all children come to school with the independent reading strategies necessary to substantially increase their vocabulary. We have to craft these experiences as well. Focusing on read-alouds ensures that children will be exposed to the power of reading through modeling and a focus on books.

The more children read, the more words they are exposed to and the more words they acquire (Allington, 2005; Nagy, 1988). But this sequence requires that you not only have reading available in your room, but that you also foster it through Independent Sustained Reading time. Independent Sustained Reading is different from Sustained Silent Reading in that Independent Sustained Reading occurs during a workshop or other class period during which children can interact with one another about their reading. The children are not silent, and they may be working toward assigned reading goals developed collaboratively with the teacher.

At first, Independent Sustained Reading is about "bottom time," or time in a chair with book in hand for 30 to 40 minutes. During this time the teacher may be meeting with small groups

Management Tips

- Creating a meeting area in your room gives students who need to move around the opportunity to get up and walk to another place.

- Gathering students in a meeting area signals to them that a different type of instruction is about to begin.

- Hanging out and building community is important to help students take risks while discussing the read-aloud and sharing their ideas about words.

- Moving students away from their desks removes the plethora of distracters in, on, and around their desks that can steal their attention.

or conferring with individual children, coaching them on decoding, fluency, or comprehension strategies. The sheer practice time of reading is important, and goals for Independent Sustained Reading can include:

■ Developing "bottom time"

■ Nurturing the ability to read fiction and nonfiction texts, comprehend them, and understand each text structure

■ Making deep and important connections to text

■ Comprehending and analyzing works by many authors and across genres

The Essence of the Lessons

■ **First, connect students to the task . . .**

Introduce the book and connect students to the vocabulary task for the day. Help the children connect to prior knowledge to speed the transition to new learning.

■ **Next, convey that reading is a pleasure . . .**

Savor the book and show the children how wonderful books are and how powerful their messages can be. Make the children believe there is nothing better than reading.

■ **Then, discuss important points . . .**

During these five or six strategically planned moments, stop reading and discuss points you are making to support your objective. Sharing may also include the teaching time that occurs immediately after reading the book.

■ **Finally, reinforce learning . . .**

Record thoughts, words, and connections on a chart to reinforce word learning and to visually reinforce the oral discussion.

For students to make deep meaning, they need to:
■ Feel that the lesson or activity is important to them
■ Feel emotionally connected to the work
■ Discover how the information connects to other things they know
■ Become immersed in the beauty of text and language

Daily Time Target for Reading Aloud

Plan to spend 15 to 20 minutes reading aloud each day from a picture book or short nonfiction source. Some books you will be able to finish in one day; others will take two days or more. When you are ready to move into chapter books, be sure to choose books that are packed with language-learning opportunities, but not so overly packed that your students lose the meaning.

The Cutting Edge of Vocabulary Acquisition

You need to choose books for read-alouds that are above the children's independent reading level, but not too far above. The perfect level is the cutting edge of their listening abilities (Stahl & Nagy, 2006). The most advanced stage of what they can comprehend when you read aloud is where you want to place your time and effort. And picture books afford many opportunities. These opportunities range from the words in the text to the precise and powerful words you can use to describe theme, plot, and the hook or lead in an article. Engaging texts like picture books, poetry, feature articles, nonfiction materials, and chapter books are filled with challenging words steeped in illustrations, plot, interesting facts, and rhythmic language. By concentrating on the cutting edge, you focus on connecting words to a text in such a way that students can grasp new meaning.

The cutting edge is found in books because that is where the words are. The richness of vocabulary comes from two features: the rare words in the text and the number of words available for children to read. It is important for children to read a lot, and to be read to. This is because as more common words are heard or read over and over, they become sight words.

Reading and being read to often is important because when we are exposed to words in a meaningful context, we acquire an understanding of those words. The most meaningful context is writing, because everything is explained or can be explored in reference materials. The words connect to ideas and information we already know.

Reading children's books is important because of the number of rare words in the text. So-called rare words are labeled "rare" because they don't appear among the 10,000 most frequent words in the language (Hayes & Ahrens, 1988). Some rare words don't really seem that rare when we hear them: *trigger, logic, reluctant, scold, cautious.* The more experiences children have with words, the more quickly they own them. You may not believe it, but children's books have twice the number of rare words as the typical conversation of two college-educated adults. It's true! Conversations between college-educated adults have an average of 17.3 rare words per 1,000 and children's books have 30.9 rare words per 1,000 (Stahl & Nagy, 2006). Reading aloud counts!

Lessons for Read-Alouds

Suggested titles are woven into each lesson description to give you an idea of how the lesson would look. Although you can choose to use these texts, you should choose a text that is comfortable for you and your students. Be careful to choose books at the correct level. Your students in fifth grade won't learn as much vocabulary from a book written for very young children, so save those for independent reading time. Reach for the beefy choices instead. Focus your read-aloud on the wonder of language and the entertainment of a good read. Drench your students in books and informational texts, and flaunt the wonderful and interesting words found in these texts around your room. See the chart below (Figure 4.5) for a list of the lessons presented in this unit of study.

The Power of Read-Alouds

Lesson 1: Listening and Learning From a Read-Aloud

Teaching Point: Focus on books read aloud to hear words and consider what they mean

Lesson 2: Inferring Word Meanings

Teaching Point: Good readers infer the meaning of unknown words by considering information in the text or pictures.

Lesson 3: Choosing Words to Describe Story Elements

Teaching Point: Words create visual images in our minds.

Lesson 4: Shaking Down a Word

Teaching Point: Develop word consciousness by paying attention to words.

Lesson 5: Describing the Hook Words in Nonfiction

Teaching Point: Focus on how combining words enhances meaning and imagery.

Figure 4.5

Listening and Learning From a Read-Aloud

Teaching Points

- Focus children on unusual ways to use words to describe objects.

- Help children consider the meaning of words.

- Build "bottom time" by establishing read-alouds as an important element of classroom culture.

Prep Tips

- Obtain a copy of *Daffodil* by Emily Jenkins (2004).

- Prepare a Color Words chart to record unusual ways to describe colors. See the chart at right (Figure 4.6) for an example.

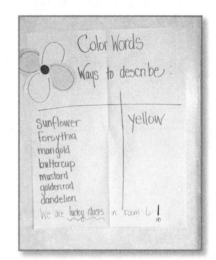

Figure 4.6: Word chart for *Daffodil*

Connect

Explain that every day the class will listen to a read-aloud and that during the read-aloud students will be involved with word learning. Tell the children that by listening to stories they are going to expand their vocabularies, so it's really important that they relax and prepare to be involved. Your introduction to this activity might sound like this: "Today we are going to begin by reading, because I love reading. When I really get involved in a book, I feel like I am on a journey and I never know exactly where the journey will end. It is exciting! Every day we will be reading books that have meaning in terms of what we are studying. Sometimes I will pick a book just because I think it is beautiful and offers language we can enjoy. Other times the book will connect to other topics in class. It is important that during the reading, you focus. I also want you to focus so you can hear the words and think about what they mean."

Read

Read *Daffodil* with enthusiasm and care. In addition to the color words, other academic words to focus on include: *squinty, dimple, different, sour, extremely,* and *shush.* An idiom that appears in the book is *lucky ducks.*

Share

"Look at the fun and interesting way Emily Jenkins uses the words that are in her book *Daffodil*. I have never seen so many ways to describe a yellow flower. She mainly uses flower names: *sunflower, forsythia, marigold, buttercup, mustard, goldenrod, black-eyed Susan, dandelion, yellow rose of Texas*. I am going to list these words on our chart. (See Figure 4.6). I am labeling the chart, 'Color Words.' Notice I put the color on the right and on the left I listed the words from the book."

Wrap-Up

"We explored many flower words today that were used in the story to make us imagine the color yellow. As you think of flowers that would describe other colors, I want you to add them to our chart."

Inferring Word Meanings

Teaching Points

■ Readers infer word meanings from other words in the sentence or paragraph.

■ Young readers infer word meanings by looking at the pictures.

Prep Tips

■ Obtain a copy of the book *Amelia and Eleanor Go for a Ride* by Pam Muñoz Ryan (1999).

■ Choose a few words from the text that would be appropriate to teach to your class.

■ Prepare chart on inferring word meanings (see Figure 4.8).

Connect

Tell the class that good readers figure out the meaning of unknown words by inferring what the words mean. Notice that students who have just begun reading chapter books, or students who are not good readers, tend to skip over difficult words. They don't go back and revisit words. By guiding children to take the necessary steps to figure out words with our help, we can help them learn to approximate word meanings with some accuracy. While these approximations

Figure 4.7: Front cover of the book *Amelia and Eleanor Go for a Ride*

don't substitute for knowing a word well, they help children gain fluency, enjoy reading, and read more words overall.

Tell the class that they are going to practice inferring word meanings together so that they can get good at the process. Together you will consider the word, think about what has happened in the story thus far, and look at the pictures for clues to the word meanings. You will also lead a discussion about the word and possible meanings. It is important to list these wonderings and deductions on a chart to help children grasp the steps and the thinking involved. Realize that only rarely do good readers stop reading to look up a word in the dictionary. Yes, we all do this from time to time, but it is not the first strategy we choose. Tell the children that by learning how to infer word meanings, they will learn many new words and be practicing the skills of a good reader.

Read

Make the reading an honored time during your day. Don't allow anyone to use the bathroom or get a drink of water (except for emergencies, or course!). When we say to children, "Oh, this book is so important and lovely, you really can't miss it," we are saying to them that it is important to us and to our classroom community that they participate in the read-aloud.

Share

During the share, you will revisit two or three words from the text. Often I prefer to interrupt my reading and explore the words right on the spot. Through open discussion children will be able to develop a good idea of a word's meaning as they tap into the understanding the other children bring to the conversation (Stahl, 1999). Words in *Amelia and Eleanor Go for a Ride* that are effective for this lesson include: *adventurous, independence, license,* and *solo.*

To guide children through the processes of inferring word meanings, ask questions that build understanding and write student responses on the meaning inferring chart below (Figure 4.8).

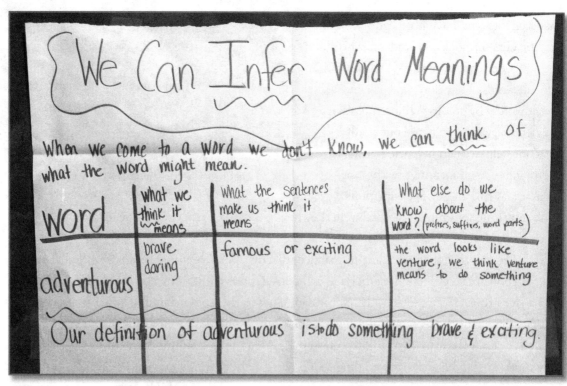

Figure 4.8: Chart on inferring word meanings

- "What do you think the word *adventurous* means?"

- "Based on the surrounding text, what might we infer that this word means?"

- "What else do we know about the word?"

If the children's ideas of a word are vague, you can help them hone a more appropriate definition. You might say something like the following:

"Perhaps we should clarify, because I think our ideas are vague. What else do we know about the word *adventurous* from the sentence? The book says, 'And when two of the most famous and adventurous women in the world got together, something exciting was bound to happen,'" (p. 3).

To encourage students to think more deeply about their proposed definition, you might say something like this: "I think we have developed a good understanding of the word *adventurous*. Let's write our definition on the chart. What should we say first?" Write the brainstormed definition on the inferring chart, then have students reflect. "How did we decide what this word meant? What did we think about first?"

Wrap-Up

"When you come across words you don't know and, because of that, you don't understand what you are reading, I want you to stop and think about what the word might mean before you go on. Remember a 'just right' book is a book in which you only make three mistakes per page when reading alone." Three mistakes per page is a ballpark estimate for children as they self-select chapter books and picture books with a lot of text. A just-right book should be about a 97 percent accuracy rate—that is, children should know 97 out of 100 words in a passage (Fountas & Pinnell, 1996).

Choosing Words to Describe Story Elements

Teaching Points

- Children develop vocabulary by discussing various story elements.

- These discussions provide safe and authentic forums for children to try out literary language.

- Children comprehend what they are reading and what is read to them by discussing the book and the book's elements.

Prep Tips

- Select books from the book list in Appendix A, and prepare them for read-aloud by using sticky notes to mark pages that feature the story element you plan to discuss.

- Create a library or favorite book basket in your classroom to store your read-aloud selections. Keep a stack of note cards or sticky notes close by to keep track of important pages in each book that reinforce your lessons.

Connect

"Books can help us think about many things and give us many opportunities to talk and explore new ideas. Sometimes if we look at how the author wrote a book, we can understand the book at a deeper level. Most storybooks have certain elements in them we call *story elements*."

Lucy Calkins defines the elements of story in her important book *The Art of Teaching Reading* (2001) as follows:

- Characters: People or animals that are believable, with real problems and issues. Some of them change over time as the story progresses.

- Setting: The time and place of the story. This is a grander picture than just the scene of the action, and includes the city or town where the story takes place.

- Plot: The sequence of events in the story. The events create plot, but may or may not be told in chronological order.

- Movement through time: Time passes in stories, and writers use various techniques to suggest the passage of time. The time is evident in the plot and often seen in the characters as they change (or don't change) with the events of the story.

■ Change: In a story, something changes. Often this is framed by a conflict, resolution, and denouement. The denouement occurs as a final wrap-up after the resolution. It helps the reader put all the pieces together and feel satisfied.

The best books for teaching plot are those that you are most comfortable discussing with children. It is important to plan ahead and choose the words you will focus on before the read-aloud. Focus on the words that are the cutting edge of your students' abilities. It is best to focus on only three or four per story so that you aren't overwhelming children with words and thus detracting from the story itself. The read-aloud titles suggested in Appendix A (pages 133–136) are just a few of my favorites for teaching vocabulary.

Read
Choose a book from the list and read it aloud. Focus on one or two story elements to discuss after reading.

Share
Comprehension lessons link to vocabulary lessons when you have in-depth discussions about story elements, including character, setting, plot, movement through time, and change (Calkins, 2001). These lessons can be as simple as a short discussion during and after a read-aloud. What is important is that the *children* do the talking after *you* model, model, model. While modeling these academic discussions, use powerful words that describe the story elements with precise language. Say the character is shifty, and then explain, "*Shifty* means he is deceptive and he lies, and he isn't honest."

Wrap-Up
Have a group discussion about one or two story elements. Ensure that all the children have a chance to voice their idea or opinion about the book and the story elements the class discusses. During the discussion write down important ideas, including important vocabulary from the book, in order to record the group's ideas.

Story elements are the structures in fiction that help us connect to and understand stories. When we discuss our thinking about story elements with a partner, we understand our reading better. Remember to use the words that describe specific elements when sharing.

Shaking Down a Word

Teaching Points

- Students brainstorm words connected to one main word.

- Thinking of a word, and the context the word is from, generates other words.

- "Shake down" the word, metaphorically, as a farmer might shake a nut tree for the season's harvest to fall to the ground.

- Focus on having the children dig deeper, or challenge their brains. The more they think, the more words they will think of.

Prep Tips

- Prepare small blank charts (8 ½ x 14) for groups to record their Semantic Map. See the examples of Semantic Maps in Appendix B (pages 144–146).

- Obtain a copy of *Sophie's Masterpiece: A Spider's Tale* by Eileen Spinelli (2001).

Semantic Map   Name _____ Date _____

Connect

"Good readers connect words to other words they know. One way to do this is by 'shaking down' a word. I think of this activity as a 'shake down' because you begin with one word and keep reaching for more words that you can associate with the main word. You 'shake down' your memory and let the words fall onto the page." Introduce the book *Sophie's Masterpiece: A Spider's Tale* by Eileen Spinelli (2001). "This is a tender story about a spider and her life's work, which goes unappreciated by people until she meets a young woman about to have a baby."

"We are going to focus on a few words in the book after we read it. I want you to think about the masterpieces Sophie makes, because when we are finished reading, we are going to talk about them. A masterpiece is a work of art that is truly beautiful." It is important to read and discuss the book first before doing the word shake-down activity as this helps students to connect to words and associate them with other words and ideas, thus learning a word to a deeper degree.

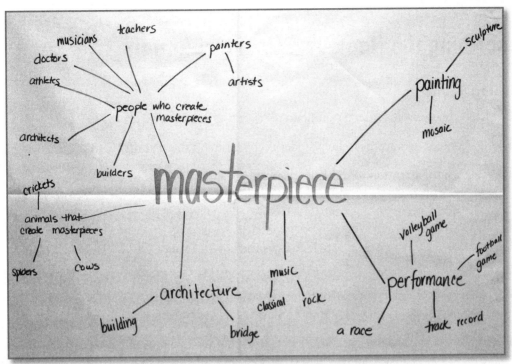

Figure 4.9: A Semantic Map for the book "Sophie's Masterpiece"

Read

While reading, pause from time to time to mention the masterpieces that Sophie is making. Have the children focus on the beauty of the work and the characters' reactions.

Share

After reading the book and discussing the children's thoughts and ideas, put a blank Semantic Map on the easel near your teaching area and write the word *masterpiece* in the middle of the map. This is the graphic organizer you will use for this shakedown activity. As the words "shake" from the children, write them on the Semantic Map. Encourage the class to begin to think about how to define *masterpiece*. The Semantic Map above shows an example of a word shake down. In this example from Melissa Jones's fifth-grade classroom in California, I asked the children to share anything that popped into their heads, even if they didn't think it was connected. By doing this, the group came to some deep "ah-ha" connections for the word *masterpiece*. The children related the word to a painting as well as to a beautiful performance by an athlete.

Wrap-Up

Have the class work in small groups to "shake down" other words from the book in small groups.

Describing the Hook Words in Nonfiction

Teaching Points

- Students choose words from a non-fiction article to discuss whole class.

- Discuss content area words to help students comprehend the text and learn words.

- Direct students' attention to the embedded meaning in print features.

Prep Tips

- Prepare copies of a nonfiction article such as the one in *Science World* (Scholastic, 2006) shown in figure 4.10.

- Use students vocabulary journals to record words from the text.

Connect

It is important to model language use and thought with informational texts. Informational texts make engaging read-alouds, and a plethora of books, journals, and magazines are available for reading to the whole class. Our children face standardized tests chock-full of nonfiction each year. It is estimated that standardized tests contain 50–85 percent nonfiction texts (Hoyt, 2002).

These content-specific texts are a gold mine for vocabulary instruction. Having in-depth discussions about ways to glean important information from texts, or simply about the pleasure of reading about interesting things is a valuable addition to our diet of picture books. Informational texts are filled with content area words, and provide multiple opportunities for exposure to new words.

When children discuss informational text, the learning moves from the elements that capture their attention to the information embedded in each line, section, and article. You can lead wonderful discussions on the meaning of feature articles, the persuasiveness of the author, the factual reality of statements, the hook of the articles (or words that draw the reader into each piece), and the details that support the main idea. The possibilities for word learning are endless.

Show children a feature article such as, "And They're Off!" by Britt Norlander (2006) which appeared in *Science World* by Scholastic (See Figure 4.10). Before reading, connect children to the piece by listing on the board two or three important vocabulary words. I choose words children need to be familiar with in order to understand the text. While many content-specific words, or Tier Three words, as Beck and her colleagues refer to them (2002), are evident in this section, I teach the content words that appear in the article. Three such words are *competition*, *endurance*, and *hormone*. Present these words to the children and discuss their meanings.

Read

Now the children are ready to have a go at their own word list. After previewing the pictures, the captions, and the heading, I have them brainstorm a word list that is related to horse racing. It is important to have the children think and talk about what they know because it engages them actively, and I can quickly see who has knowledge about horse racing and who doesn't. During reading, I stop and discuss content words that seem confusing. Many times with content words preteaching isn't necessary, as the context of the article teaches the word. For example, the simplest way to teach the word *thoroughbred* is to just say, "They're a breed of horses that make especially fast racehorses." Because the article provides so much context for the word *thoroughbred*, I can spend time teaching other words like *gallop, stride, tissue,* or *sprinter*.

Figure 4.10

Share

After reading, the children revisit their list and put a checkmark beside the words they connect with horseracing. Encourage them to add new words. Share a few of these words with the whole class.

Wrap-Up

Have the children record a few new words they learned from the article, and the definition of these words, in their word journals or on a Just-Right Word List Record Sheet (page 142, Appendix B).

The Cutting Edge of Vocabulary Acquisition

The cutting edge is the most advanced stage that children can comprehend when you read aloud.

Choose read-aloud books just above the children's reading abilities.

Picture books offer a plethora of opportunities because they are where the words are!

"Word learning" occurs when we read, read, read aloud to children.

CHAPTER 5

Getting to the Power of Words

How Focusing on Teaching Concepts Accelerates Students' Word Learning

"Right," you might be thinking. "This is a book about teaching words, and I'm supposed to teach concepts instead?" Don't let this idea confuse you. Words and concepts are inextricably linked.

When teaching vocabulary well, we don't teach words, we teach concepts *about* words. The words are little hangtags that attach to the concepts that our brain acquires. Those hangtags are labels for thoughts, feelings, sensations, ideas, and information, and they are interconnected to other ideas, thoughts, and information stored in our memories. But that is the complicated way of looking at things; let me simplify the idea.

While typing this chapter, I am drinking coffee from a cup that has the word *RELAX* in capital letters on the outside rim. When I see the word, I don't think of the caffeine I am consuming, I see myself sitting back in my chair, putting my feet up on the edge of my desk, and enjoying the coffee. Sometimes when I see the word *Relax* on the cup, I think of lying around the house and reading a book, or I see myself stopping to breathe for a moment in my bustling day. What I don't see in my mind is a dictionary definition. According to the Encarta dictionary on my computer, the word *relax* has six definitions: to spend time at ease; to make or become less tense; to make or become less strict; to become or make something looser; to make or become less intense; and to straighten hair.

When we teach a concept about the word, we are teaching students to connect the hangtag of a word to information, or to memory. Memory and learning are intertwined, and memory is what enables us to learn by experience (Wolfe, 2001). So, by discussing context, ideas, situations, and information about words, we are discussing the concepts the words represent—and helping students learn.

Let's give this idea a spin. On a piece of paper, list the words that come to mind when you read the word in the box below.

Refresh

This word is from another cup in my collection; does knowing that fact change your perception of the word? Can you think of more words to write down now that you are thinking of *refresh* in conjunction with a coffee cup?

The interesting thing about words is how they connect to our memories. When I see *refresh* on my coffee cup, I think of different images than I do for the word *relax*. In the school district for which I work "refresh" is the name we gave to our plan for purchasing new technology. My school computer is referred to as a "refresh" computer. So, when I see *refresh*, I think of computers because that is what I associate the word with in my memory.

Word Wizards All!

When we truly know a word, we instantly know what it means when we hear it or see it in print. It takes longer for us to choose the best way to state a definition of a word than it takes to recall what a word means. This is strange, but true; think of a word you are very familiar with, and then reflect on how long it took you to think of what the word means. I am thinking of the word *joke*. I thought of the meaning of that word instantly. Now when I think of a definition, I had to pause and think for a moment of the best way to define *joke*, even though I know the word well.

When I see a word in print that I don't know, the process in my brain is a completely different story. Usually, at first I draw a blank and think *What??? Maybe I can just skip it!* Most times, I try to focus on the word (I am the teacher, after all, and I have to model word learning for students!). If I come across a word that I am not as familiar with, *witticism*, for example, I pause and think of connections that might help me understand what the word means (assuming I didn't skip it, of course!). I might look at parts of the word, the sentence, and the sentences before and after the word. I do this automatically, and only when I am really desperate do I reach for a dictionary. This process is what good readers and word sleuths do often; it is the process that we need our students hooked into as well.

This unit of study focuses on the three levels of knowing words: association level, comprehension level, and generation level (Blachowicz & Fisher, 2000; Stahl, 1999). Chapter 7 discusses these levels in depth and the research behind them, but for now, we will focus on the application of these word knowledge levels in your classroom. According to Steven Stahl (1985), the three levels of word *knowing* can be seen in the classroom when students have word associations, word comprehension, and word generation.

Word Association

- Recognize words they read or hear

- Have curiosity about new words

- Are able to attend to new words, rather than forgetting them immediately

Word Comprehension

- Know and understand words they read or hear

- Can answer multiple-choice test questions about a word

- Appreciate beautiful language

Word Generation

- Use words in writing

- Use words in conversation and academic discussion

- Use words in new ways

Deepen Learning by Focusing on Concepts

This unit assumes that children have developed a love of word consciousness during the first few weeks of school. They find, explore, and use words that are charged with meaning. This unit also assumes that children have been read to daily for several weeks and are involved in daily Independent Sustained Reading. Children who are ready for delving deeper into meaning are word lovers and word sleuths. They seek out words with verve and share these words with great excitement as they uncover new meaning, or they may be quiet sleuths who slip powerful words into their writing like secret packages, not bringing attention to themselves until their piece is read.

These students are ready for intense instruction that probes at deep connections between ideas and words. This is instruction that focuses on the concepts attached to those little hangtags in our memories called words.

About the Unit

Shifting from a focus on word consciousness to a focus on word contexts and definitions means children will be flexing their thinking muscles. Unfortunately that's a "muscle group" that is often difficult for students to flex. Thinking deeply is hard; children might often find themselves wishing to fill in a blank on a worksheet or work in a group and let someone else do the thinking and talking rather than give their thinking muscles a workout. This is a normal feeling that children have, and you may hear them grumble, "Oh, this is too hard." When these little rumblings start, smile and tell them that you *know* they can do it. And be careful; don't let these complaints throw your teaching goals off track. Work with your class to help them think about their own learning. Perhaps they might list ideas to encourage their own "brain muscle" flexing. A poster might look like this:

We Work Our Brain Muscles Together

- Think of what a word looks like in your mind.

- Tell your partner about the image in your mind when you hear a word.

- Don't give up and say, "I dunno . . . "

- When your brain hurts from thinking, rest a bit, and then think again.

- No thought or idea about a word is silly.

- We share our ideas about words to make all of us smart!

Figure 5.1

By going deeper, all children in your class will have the opportunity to flex their thinking muscles and therefore develop larger vocabularies. Being able to use a word in writing or when speaking takes a greater understanding of a word's meaning. A few routines accelerate students' ability to focus deeply on word learning. Children need to be active learners, hooked into visual and kinesthetic modalities, exposed to words multiple times in authentic ways (in other words, *not* looking up definitions and memorizing for the test on Friday), and focused on contextual and definitional explanations (Beck et al., 2002; Nagy & Scott, 2000). For this unit, think:

Active

In each lesson, children thrive when they work with partners (Perry, Turner, & Meyer, 2006). All too often we rush children to be independent and don't trust that they can learn when working with a partner or small group. Slow down your teaching and give them a bit of time to work on ideas with a peer. If you set up partner expectations at the beginning of the year, the children will know the game plan and be able to get to work quickly. You may be surprised at what they can do together.

Visual/Kinesthetic

A picture is worth 1,000 words . . . For memory making this is literally true. We encourage children to visually imprint new concepts by writing information down. By writing, they create a visual picture that supports memory. Remember that our goal is to move information into long-term memory where it can be stored *and* retrieved (Marzano, 2004; Stahl & Stahl, 2004). Acting out words, having children demonstrate a definition, also supports children to remember what a word means.

Repetition

If you thought you did a great job helping a child out last week by quickly explaining a word on the fly (or when she asked, "What does this word mean?"), you probably just added a small amount of information to the total picture she will develop about that word. That one-time definition is a small stone in a large pool. Some researchers estimate it takes at least 12 purposeful encounters with a word for children to *own* it, or have the word become part of their generative vocabulary. Generative vocabulary refers to words you can retrieve from memory and use correctly (Stahl,

1985; Stahl & Nagy, 2006). Just remember: drill exercises are proven by research to be the *least* effective way to teach vocabulary, so every opportunity you provide for a child to experience, think about, and play with a word is another small pebble in the pool. But those pebbles have ripple effects, and the repeated exposure amounts to a whole lot of learning.

■ Background

When working beyond Fast Mapping a word (see Fast Mapping below and in Chapter 7), children need to work with context and a definition to understand what a word means and how it is used. They will think of images that match a word's meaning, and with time they will bring together the definitions they have heard and create their own (Stahl & Nagy, 2006).

Fast Mapping

Fast Mapping is the unconscious action our memory takes when we first begin to learn a word. In short, our brains create a meaning structure for new words very quickly. When we first learn a word, our brains have only part of a word meaning mapped in memory. We fill in the context of the word slowly with repeated exposures to the word (Carey, 1978). While it takes an undetermined amount of time for our memories to acquire all the necessary information and context for a word, Fast Mapping occurs quickly and gives us structures to hang new information on in our memory.

Fast Mapping is part of explicit vocabulary instruction. Children who think about words and actively participate in the process of Fast Mapping will be able to remember words better and expand their vocabularies at a faster rate. When children first encounter a word, we can accelerate their learning of that word by connecting them to it, helping them discover a context, and guiding them to think about the word's meaning.

Maintaining the Cutting Edge of Word Learning

Going deeper with explicit instruction pushes children to the learning curve, where they think and use vocabulary in new ways. If the cutting edge is the most advanced stage of what students can comprehend when you read aloud (see Chapter 4), then the cutting edge of explicit instruction is the most advanced stage of word use the children can comprehend and access with support. The cutting edge is supported by choosing the most appropriate words for explicit instruction (Blachowicz & Fisher, 2000).

The Magic 8 Word List: A Perfect Number for Explicit Word Instruction

William Nagy and Richard Anderson's (1984) research estimates that texts from grades 3 to 9 have approximately 88,500 distinct word families. It is not possible for you to focus on this large number during one school year. Fortunately, many words are acquired during free reading. This is a great reason to create a classroom where reading occurs daily for at least 30 minutes. The large number of distinctive word families also points to the importance of focusing your weekly word list. You want to purposely teach words, not clutter up your curriculum. Current literature recommends teaching eight to ten words per week (Beck, McKeown, & Kucan, 2002). Focusing on eight words works well because you can easily teach eight words each week with 15 minutes a day. You can break word learning into four days of instruction, teaching two words each day, and keeping one day for conferring and assessment. The Magic 8 words don't disappear, however, after a five-day focus. These words should become part of word walls and word banks in your classroom. The photo below (Figure 5.2) and those on the next two pages (Figure 5.3–5.6) show how different teachers created word banks from words they taught each week.

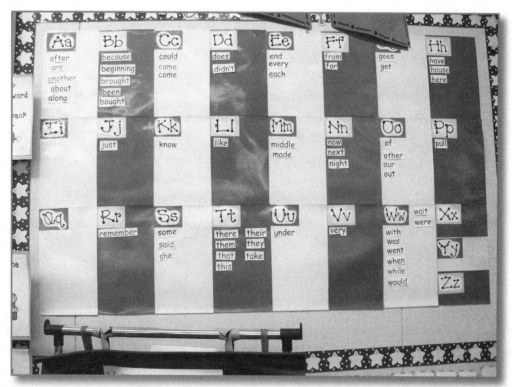

Figure 5.2: This wall lists high-frequency words.

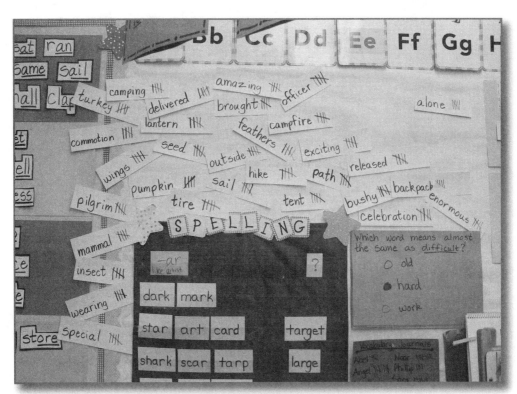

Figure 5.3: A word wall can incorporate many examples of words the class has studied.

Figure 5.4: A pocket chart works well for a word bank.

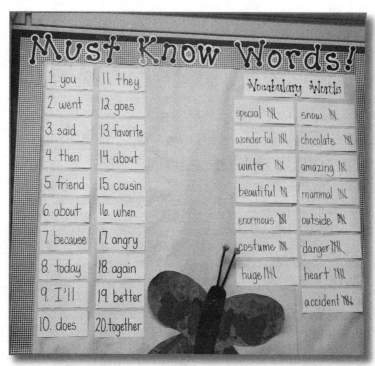

Figure 5.5: Here's a second-grade spelling word bank and vocabulary word bank side by side.

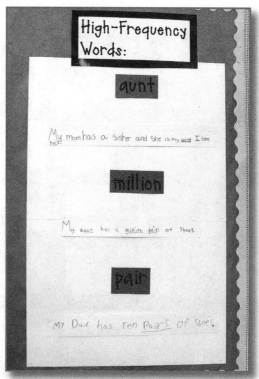

Figure 5.6: This simple word bank lists the words and student written sentences.

Accelerated Vocabulary Instruction

Because the words are important, the children can record the weekly words themselves and then keep the word lists in a folder. A Magic 8 word list (see Figure 5.7) should provide a simple way for children to record and refer to weekly words. Definitions can be added to other graphic organizers that can accompany the word list. Organizational tools that work well for teaching vocabulary include vocabulary folders where children can file the Magic 8 word lists, vocabulary journals where the words can be copied, and personal word dictionaries, where children keep their Magic 8 words and accompanying graphic pages in a three-hole-punched folder or binder. A full-size reproducible of the Magic 8 word list is on page 143 in Appendix B. Sources for word lists include:

- *For the Love of Words: Vocabulary Instruction That Works* (Paynter, Bodrova, & Doty, 2005)

- *Words Their Way* (Bear, Invernizzi, Templeton, & Johnston, 2003)

- *Word Study Lessons: Letters, Words, and How They Work: Grade 3* (Pinnell & Fountas, 2004)

Going Deeper With Word Concepts

Supporting children as they comprehend and access new words means pushing, *just a little,* but ensuring that while teaching you think in these terms (see pages 72–73 for a review):

- Active
- Visual/Kinesthetic
- Repetition
- Background

Teach specific words by focusing on:

♦ Synonyms for words students already know

♦ Words that students already know but that have multiple meanings

♦ Words that represent new concepts in content area textbooks

♦ Words that you discuss and analyze during or after read-alouds

Name _____

Magic 8!

1. special
2. wonderful
3. beautiful
4. amazing
5. colorful
6. unique
7. peculiar
8. different

143

Figure 5.7: Example of a Magic 8 list

What Going Deeper With Word Meanings Can Do for Children:

- Provide an array of word-learning strategies instead of relying on only one or two

- Provide modeling of the proper use of dictionaries so children can match an appropriate definition with a word use in context

- Develop figurative language

- Expose them to a large variety of words

Going Deeper With Word-Learning Vocabulary Lessons

The array of lessons in this unit is organized by context-building lessons, or definition-building lessons. Unlike the first two units of study presented in chapters 3 and 4, which list the lessons in a suggested order, in this unit you can pick and choose from the list of lessons. The purpose of this unit of study is to guide the children in your class to deeper meaning. These lessons are part of your Fab Fifteen. Remember to focus on the design of effective mini-lessons presented in Chapter 3. Effective mini-lessons have four parts: connect, teach, practice, and wrap-up. See figure 5.8 for suggested teaching points in this unit.

Going Deeper: Lessons Focused on Context

Lesson 1: Lassoing Imagery: Teaching Meaning With Mind Pictures
Teaching Point: Develop definitions of a focus word by connecting images and words together.

Lesson 2: Defining Words With Images Using Word Maps
Teaching Point: Organize word attributes, images and description in sequence on a semantic map.

Lesson 3: Mapping Word Meaning
Teaching Point: Focus on images and descriptions that define a word in a four square map.

Lesson 4: Learning Word Concepts Through Categories
Teaching Point: Categorize words to deepen student understanding of word meanings.

Lesson 5: Learning Word Meanings Through Compare and Contrast
Teaching Point: Compare and contrast word concepts with Venn diagrams.

Lesson 6: Teaching Concepts Through Comparisons
Teaching Point: Focus on synonyms and the subtle differences between words.

Lesson 7: Make a Difference With Word Journals
Teaching Point: By recording words, children remember word meaning and connections to other words.

Lesson 8: Making Dictionaries Count
Teaching Point: Examine word context in order to select the correct dictionary definition.

Lesson 9: Conveying What's Interesting About Word Parts
Teaching Point: Learn how word parts affect word roots. Use word parts to decode and understand word meanings.

Figure 5.8

Lassoing Imagery: Teaching Meaning With Mind Pictures

Teaching Points

- Connect images and words to a focus word by recording thoughts on a Semantic Map.

- Focus on the multiple images to describe words.

- Develop a deeper understanding of a word by discussing shades of meaning with the whole class.

Prep Tips

- Prepare current weekly Magic 8 word list (see page 143).

- Prepare overhead transparency of Semantic Map, or draw a large map on a sheet of chart paper (see Figure 5.9).

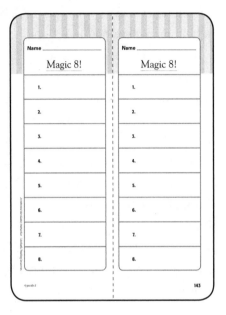

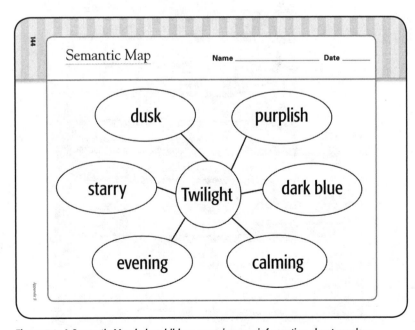

Figure 5.9: A Semantic Map helps children organize new information about words.

79

Lesson Focus

Images are created from the schema children have about a word. When we talk or read aloud, children *see* in their minds what we are presenting verbally. Then, as they hear more information, children's schema will become more developed. Children with limited vocabularies may have limited schema. They may lack multiple words to describe existing images in memory, so we have to help them develop these ideas.

To begin the lesson, I write the target word in the middle circle and prepare the children to listen carefully. "When I say a word, a flood of pictures enters my mind. Sometimes I lock on one picture, or mental image, that helps me see a word meaning clearly." Next, I prepare them for how they will do the same technique. "Close your eyes. When I say a word, I want you to focus on the picture that comes into your head. Focus on it well because you are going to describe the picture to the person sitting next to you. Ready . . . ." I state one of the words from my Magic 8 weekly word list and I wait. Since the word is somewhat unfamiliar to the students, I let them think a bit before continuing. "If anyone has a picture in their head about the meaning of the word, show thumbs up." Then I call on one student with his thumb up to share the mental image he visualizes. If no one has a mental image for the word, I share one or two of my own and hope I've primed their thinking pumps. I write the words the students use to describe the focus word in bubbles around the target word. (See Figure 5.9.)

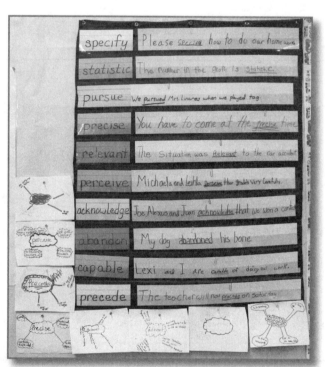

Displaying student word maps beside their list of vocabulary words helps them focus on word concepts and word meanings.

Accelerated Vocabulary Instruction

Defining Words With Images Using Word Maps

Teaching Point

- Organize word attributes, images, and description in sequence on a Word Map.

Prep Tips

- Copy the Word Map from Appendix B (page 149) on a transparency.

- Make one copy of the Word Map for each child.

Lesson Focus

Children develop a deeper understanding of a word's meaning when they describe what the word means and then sketch an example of it. A Word Map, like the one here, helps children develop meaning by connecting ideas of what the word means to images of the word and to a fine-tuned example of the word. (Schwartz & Raphael, 1985; Stahl & Nagy, 2006). Word Maps work best when teaching abstract words such as: *friendship*, *calm*, *extreme*, *happiness*, *freedom*, *justice*, and *responsibility*.

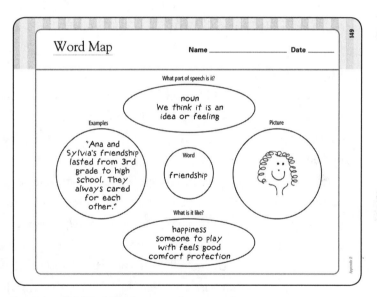

Figure 5.10: This Word Map focuses on four categories.

First, you will want your students to learn how the Word Map works; later during the year you can assign Word Maps as group work. To model, work together as a class and help children describe what the word *is*, as well as what it is *like*. Notice in the example in Figure 5.10 how the four categories are laid out around the word. Start at the top of the graphic and move clockwise around the organizer. First, discuss with the class what part of speech the word is, and then write the appropriate term (noun, verb, adjective, etc.) in the bubble. Next, move to the right-hand side of the graphic and draw a quick sketch of the word's meaning, or paste pictures from a magazine or clip art program. Then, move to the bottom bubble and write in the words the children suggest to describe the word. Finally, move to the left and ask for one or two examples of the word in a sentence. These sentences should clearly reflect the word's meaning.

Mapping Word Meaning

Teaching Points

- Organize word learning into a four-square map.

- Focus on images describing a word and images that are non-examples of a word.

- Have students write their own definition of a word's meaning.

Prep Tip

- Have legal-size blank paper handy or make photocopies of the Four-Square Word Map (page 140 in Appendix B).

Lesson Focus

The Four-Square Word Map is based on an idea by Eeds and Cockrum (1985). This simple variation of Word Maps works well in a pinch. You can use the reproducible template or just take a piece of paper (the bigger the better for displaying on the walls) and fold it in half two times to make four squares.

I prefer students to complete Four-Square Word Maps in teams or with a partner, as they learn many more concepts working together than they can dream up on their own. Later, children can independently fill out a blank reproducible to help them remember words to prepare for analogy or definition tests they may choose to create (Stahl & Nagy, 2006).

To begin creating the map, I write the target word in the first box. If the children are completely unfamiliar with the word, I give them the word in a sentence, read a sentence or two from the primary source where I found the word, or give one or two example sentences using my own definition of the word.

Next, in the second box, I list images that come to mind. I want children to share all the ideas and words that pop into their heads when they think of the target word. In the fourth box, I write words, phrases, and ideas that are *non-examples* of the target word. I don't recommend that you explicitly teach the concept of antonyms here; non-examples and opposite concepts are not necessarily antonyms. Have the children focus on their images of the opposite idea. It is the *image* that is important here, as this is a *concept*-focused lesson, not a *definition*-focused lesson.

Then, as the children construct their own definition of the word, I write this class-written definition in the third box. Last, I return to the first box and read a dictionary definition of the target word. I have the children write this definition down and we compare our definition to the dictionary definition.

The figure below (5.11) shows an example of a Four-Square Word Map for the word *soothing*. The key to the four-square map is having the children write their own definition of the word after listing three or four examples and non-examples of the target word (Stahl & Nagy, 2006).

1. Write the target word here. (Revisit this square at the end and write down the dictionary definition.)

2. Solicit examples of the concept and write them here.

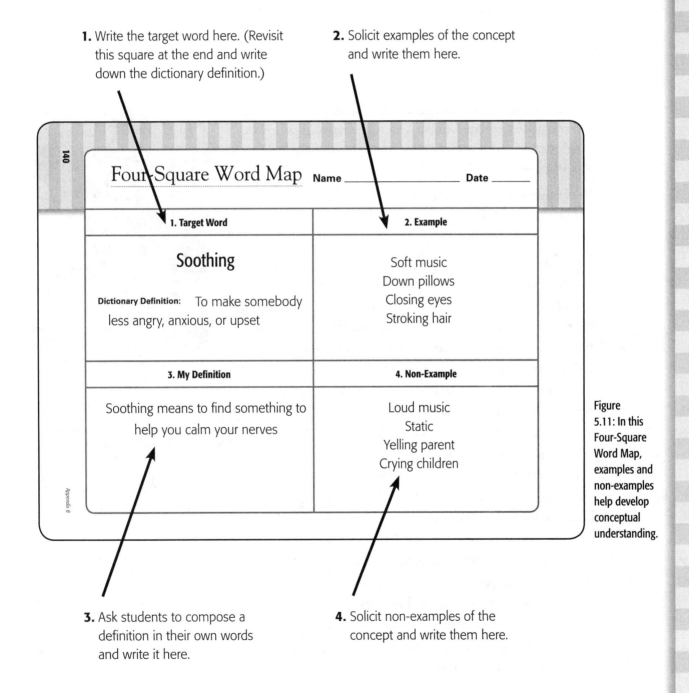

Four-Square Word Map   Name _____ Date _____

1. Target Word	2. Example
Soothing **Dictionary Definition:** To make somebody less angry, anxious, or upset	Soft music Down pillows Closing eyes Stroking hair
3. My Definition	4. Non-Example
Soothing means to find something to help you calm your nerves	Loud music Static Yelling parent Crying children

140

Appendix B

Figure 5.11: In this Four-Square Word Map, examples and non-examples help develop conceptual understanding.

3. Ask students to compose a definition in their own words and write it here.

4. Solicit non-examples of the concept and write them here.

Learning Word Concepts Through Categories

Teaching Points

- Categorize words to deepen student understanding of word meanings.

- Focus on character traits as a beginning point for categorizing words.

Prep Tips

- Prepare sorting grids. Choose a two-square or four-square grid. (See template for Four-Category Sort on page 139 in Appendix B; for working with younger children, use the Two-Category Sort on page 138.)

- Obtain copy of *Beware of the Storybook Wolves* by Lauren Child (2001).

Lesson Focus

A simple way to begin teaching the difference between word concepts is by categorizing words. A sorting grid like the one below works well to start students thinking about categories. For young children or for English learners, it is easier to start with a two-category grid (see Figure 5.14); more advanced students can work with the four-box chart. While categories can stem from any idea you explore in class, this lesson focuses on using books and categorizing character traits.

A favorite book of mine for teaching categories to primary-grade children is *Beware of the Storybook Wolves* by Lauren Child because it teems with wonderful descriptive words. Read the book first so that the children can enjoy the story and laugh at the ending. Then, discuss the characters in the book with the class and choose four to insert into the four-category sort. During your Fab Fifteen, focus on the words that

Figure 5.12: *Beware of the Storybook Wolves*

Four-Category Sort	Name _____ Date _____
Category:	Category:
Category:	Category:

describe the characters. This lesson gives examples for discussing the wicked fairy, Herb, the fairy godmother, and the wolves. "Now tell me, what did you think of the Wicked Fairy? Was she bossy . . . or nice . . . or friendly? How would you describe her?" As the children brainstorm words that describe the character, write them in the appropriate place on the chart. A character chart can be simple and look something like Figure 5.13:

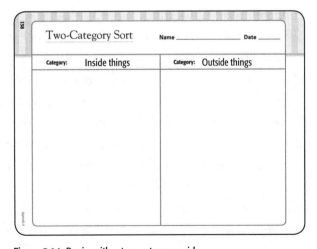

Figure 5.13: This sorting grid focuses on four categories.

The information in this brainstormed chart can quickly develop into a comparison chart as children notice the similarities and differences among characters. You can assign any category for the sort depending on the lesson you are presenting.

Word categories work very well for expanding the vocabularies of English learners. Children can use picture cards to sort objects (and related words) into categories (Paynter, Bodrova & Doty, 2005; Stahl & Nagy, 2006). For a word/object/picture sort, begin with two categories (see Figure 5.14). English learners would take picture cards and place them on the correct side of the chart. This example is for sorting "inside things" and "outside things," but you can choose any category that makes sense with objects or pictures you have available. Another way to teach concept/word categories is to have children draw pictures and then label the pictures.

Figure 5.14: Begin with a two-category grid.

Learning Word Meanings Through Compare and Contrast

Teaching Point

- Compare and contrast word concepts with Venn diagrams.

Prep Tips

- Draw a two-circle Venn diagram on a large piece of chart paper. Label one side "Synonyms" and the other side "Antonyms."

- Obtain a copy of *Esperanza Rising* by Pam Muñoz Ryan (2002).

Lesson Focus

Students in upper grades can take categorization a step further by comparing and contrasting two different concepts, like antonyms and synonyms, or subtle differences between word meanings. While in the previous lesson I began by recording the children's thoughts about character traits, in a compare-and-contrast lesson I begin by brainstorming. I discuss with the children a word, its meaning, and different word concepts that arise through the conversation. Notice

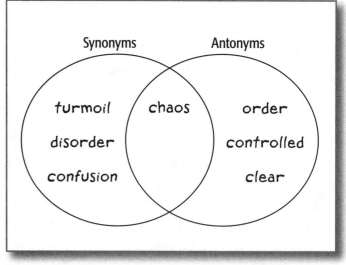

Figure 5.15: Venn diagrams help compare and contrast word concepts.

this Venn diagram (Figure 5.15) that children brainstormed for the word *chaos*. Often, when comparing and contrasting I take words from books the students are currently reading. I do this because the book gives context to an unknown word, and by reading the book, then checking a thesaurus or dictionary, the group can better understand the meaning of the unknown word.

A simple way to compare and contrast ideas is with a Venn diagram. You can develop a compare-and-contrast chart using words directly from the text, or words that describe the theme. When I use a word that isn't in the text but that states the theme of the work or describes the author's message, I use words from the text on the chart to tie the discussion and thinking back to the book. A simple Venn diagram comparing and contrasting synonyms and antonyms of an unknown word is easy to create and easy for your students to fill in. Notice that in this Venn diagram the target word is in the middle, the synonyms are on the left, and the antonyms are on the right.

You can also use a Venn diagram to develop vocabulary around concepts and themes. Because I want children to develop deep meaning about words, I tend to pick two words that are closely related, thereby stimulating discussion about how to choose between similarities and differences.

In preparation for a fifth-grade social studies unit on immigration, I read *Esperanza Rising* by Pam Muñoz Ryan with a group of students. *Esperanza Rising* is a novel about a girl who leaves her life in Mexico behind for political refuge in California. I encouraged the children to connect words and ideas to the theme of the book and learn new word definitions while doing so. Having a sense of home is one of the themes running through the book, so I encouraged the group to compare and contrast the places that Esperanza lived. The conversation was important; however, my real goal was to have the students use new vocabulary in their discussion.

"Now that we have read part of the book, we can see Esperanza struggling to carry the burden of making a home for herself and her mother in the U.S. That makes me think about her home in Mexico. What words could we use to describe the idea of home?" I listed the students' ideas on the left side of the Venn diagram (See Figure 5.17 below.) "I want you to think of her life in California. I have written this new word, *refuge*, on our chart. I think perhaps her home in California is a refuge."

"What's that?" Lupe asked.

"A refuge is a place to go when you are in danger, or have a problem. It is a place to feel safe," I explained. "Let's think about what we know about where Esperanza is staying in California. How would you describe it?" Then I listed their ideas under the word *refuge*. Along the bottom I wrote the class-generated definition of the word *refuge*.

Figure 5.16: *Esperanza Rising*

Figure 5.17: Class Venn diagram

Teaching Concepts Through Comparisons

Teaching Points

- Take the categorization lesson to new depths by focusing on synonyms and the subtle differences between words.

- Use synonyms to describe what a word means.

- Show students how words can change on a continuum from one idea to an opposite idea. This is called a linear array.

Prep Tips

- Prepare a linear array chart. See Figure 5.19 for an example.

- Read *Tulip Sees America* (1998) by Cynthia Rylant before teaching this lesson.

Figure 5.18: *Tulip Sees America*

Lesson Focus

I begin this lesson by telling the children how important it is to know many words. "Paying attention to the slight differences between words helps us expand the number of words we know. The great thing about that expansion is we get smarter! I want to show you one way to get smarter. You can do this by lining up words you know on a continuum, or a line, which goes from one idea to another." Give the students an example. Write the word *blistering* on the chalkboard or sheet of chart paper on the far left-hand side. Write the word *freezing* on the opposite side of the paper or board. Then draw five to six spaces in between the words as shown here.

Blistering _____ _____ _____ _____ _____ _____ Freezing
scorching   hot   warm   cool   icy   chilly
Write other words on the lines that describe
conditions between the two words.

Figure 5.19: Learning temperature related words through a Linear Array

Say this to the class: "Often we use a synonym in our writing because it makes our writing powerful, but we have to be careful because words have shades of meaning and can mean slightly different things. Cynthia Rylant is my favorite author, and she uses many powerful words in her writing. Powerful words make writing more specific and interesting. She uses words with a particular shade of meaning." In this lesson I would refer to one of Cynthia's books filled with powerful words; *Tulip Sees America* is particularly effective.

Read the book to the class. Before reading you might say, "When I am reading, if you hear a word you think is powerful, or unusual in how it provides description, give me a thumbs up and I will write the word on the chart."

When you try this with your class, students may list many words from the book including: *homebodies, serene, fairyland, vast, ominous, freedom, strange, salamanders,* and *cliff.* They may also list phrases: *a stand of firs, one great long breath, puffed like an old man, earth dropped away.* Write the words across the top of the chart. After reading the book, choose three or four words to place on the linear array. Choose these words with the class and then write them on the left side of the chart. Your chart should resemble the example below.

Linear Array

for *Tulip Sees America* by Cynthia Rylant and Lisa Desimini

Choose five words from the book and write them on the left side of the chart.

Word One	_____	_____	_____	_____	_____	Antonym
Word two	_____	_____	_____	_____	_____	Antonym
Word three	_____	_____	_____	_____	_____	Antonym
Word four	_____	_____	_____	_____	_____	Antonym
Word five	_____	_____	_____	_____	_____	Antonym

Figure 5.20: Synonym Array for *Tulip Sees America*

Then say: "I am always curious about an author's word choice, which helps me better understand the meaning of what I am reading. Let's take the word *vast,* for instance. I wonder how it differs from one of its synonyms, *huge.*" I write *vast* on the far left side of my linear array chart and I pull out my thesaurus. I keep several thesauruses at hand, because most that are available for adults aren't accessible to many children, and some of the children's thesauruses don't offer examples for all words.

Before I delve into thesaurus work with the children, I choose an antonym and write it on the opposing side of the line. In this example we are working with *vast,* so I choose to write *tiny* on the far right side of the chart. Sometimes you have to guide the class to the correct word category in the dictionary or thesaurus. I find it best to talk through this step with the students. "Okay, everyone, we have a decision to make. *Vast* has two categories—'large' or 'expansive.' Which do you think Cynthia Rylant was referring to? If we choose *expansive,* some of the synonyms would be *broad, far-flung, wide, spacious, ample,* and *far-reaching.* Let's reread the sentence and try to get a clue about the meaning of *vast* in this book."

After working with the word *vast,* turn the children's attention to filling in the blanks between *vast* and *tiny.* It is easiest to use two or three brainstormed words, including synonyms for *vast* and *tiny.* Write these on the spaces between the end words. When teaching an array with a picture book as a springboard, I have the class write a statement about why they think Cynthia Rylant chose *vast* over another word. I add this statement to the chart, of course! A class statement might look something like this: "We think Cynthia Rylant chose to use the word *vast* to describe Nebraska's skies in *Tulip Sees America* because she wrote that the character felt tiny, and her small car felt even tinier. *Vast* describes the feeling of something being so spacious that you feel very, very small."

Making a Difference With Word Journals

Teaching Points

- Children record thoughts and connections about words.

- Taking notes helps children remember.

- Word journals are active personal dictionaries that include words, connections between words, and sketches to remember word meanings.

Prep Tips

- Prepare a notebook or folder for each child to use only for vocabulary learning.

- Make photocopies of the Just-Right Word List recording sheet (see page 141 in Appendix B).

Just-Right Word List	Name _____ Date _____

Lesson Focus

A wonderful result of children working with words regularly and intensely is the growing attention that settles over your classroom. Children pay attention to nuances of words and how they can use specific words to convey precise meaning when talking and writing. The next step is giving the children a place to write words down that reaches beyond a list. A word journal is just the thing.

A word journal is a personal learning tool in which children record their own thoughts and connections about words and give their "thinking muscles" a workout. Each child is responsible for writing down his or her own connections and ideas. Of course, having children copy the class-brainstormed examples is important, but to have children begin to truly understand a word, they need to jot down their own notes.

An effective word journal has pages for children to write lists of words that they discover and find wondrous. It should also have pages that organize thinking. Children need a place to record words, their thoughts, word maps, and the definitions they collect. Word journals work well, but they need to be structured for deep meaning rather than merely being a superficial place to write

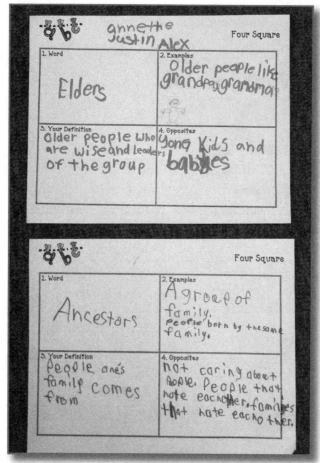

Young children can use Word Maps as journal entries to help them learn word meanings. These two examples are from a third-grade classroom.

definitions (Marzano, 2004; Marzano, Pickering, & Pollack, 2001). I like to think of primary-grade children focusing on a "just right" word list. The words in their journals are neither too hard nor too easy.

All children benefit from organizing the words in their journal. When the words are organized, children can refer back to them for application. One way to help children organize words independently is to use a Just-Right Word List recording sheet (pictured on previous page). This sheet can be run off and put in the vocabulary folder or glued into a word journal. This simple chart helps children remember the basic building blocks of learning new words: spelling, visual example, and definition.

Older students can use the Magic 8 word list. For these students, the journal becomes the place where they copy the words, write their own definitions after whole-class instruction on the word, and when appropriate, sketch a picture of the word's meaning. If children are ready, they can also include synonyms and antonyms. Rather than just creating meaningless lists of synonyms, I like children to think of an example and write a non-example in their own words. Then they can choose synonyms or an antonym that illustrates the word meaning.

Making Dictionaries Count

Teaching Point

- Examine word context in order to select the correct dictionary definition.

Prep Tips

- Have numerous student dictionaries and "grown-up" dictionaries available. Some student dictionaries don't provide enough information, and the more exposure children have to the wealth of knowledge in dictionaries, the better.

- Make copies of the Be a Word Specialist! Card (page 148 in Appendix B).

Lesson Focus

Dictionaries are great word-learning resources when we use them correctly. Using dictionaries for quiet down time, busy work, or discipline (as in "Copy all of the words from page 574 instead of going to recess . . .") is truly unproductive. Children have to flex their thinking muscles to use a dictionary properly. Dictionaries and thesauruses need to move from their places as door stoppers onto desktops where kids use them to discuss, ponder, and actively search out word meanings.

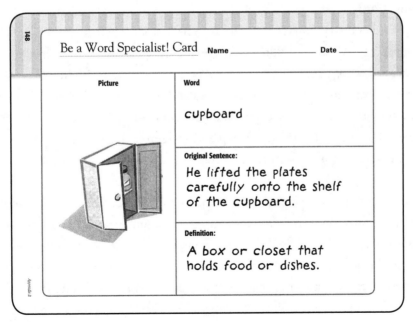

Figure 5.21: Be a Word Specialist! Card sample

Our old methods of having students look up dictionary definitions is not a strategy supported by research (Stahl & Nagy, 2006). For one thing, children haven't learned the meanings of the words they are looking up, so choosing a correct word meaning and using that meaning to comprehend text is a gamble. Sometimes they get it right and sometimes they don't, and most of the time they aren't making meaning from this activity so they just forget the word anyway. Also, when we ask children to write sentences from dictionary definitions they've copied, we usually get this type of sentence: "The *evulsion* was difficult." Do you know what *evulsion* means from the context of this sentence? Would you think I know what it means based on that sentence? I call these the "My teacher assigned 20 words so I have to look them up and write these dumb sentences" variety of sentences. *Evulsion* has little meaning to me as well. It was on the Word of the Day Web site on August 3, 2006, and as you can see, I failed to acquire this word! The definition of the noun *evulsion* is "a forcible extraction."

Avoid these perils of dictionary use by focusing on the power of combining thinking and discussion with examining dictionary definitions (Bear & Helman, 2003; Blachowicz & Fisher, 1996; Graves & Watts-Taffe, 2002). First, expect children to talk about word meanings. It is best to discuss word meanings with the whole class, pointing out multiple meanings, roots, and other significant attributes of a word. Second, have children work in groups to create worthwhile sentences that carry meaning and that help children move from the association level of word recognition to the comprehension level—or better yet, to the generation level of word use! (Beck et al., 2003). It helps to have print in the room that familiarizes children with the functions of dictionaries and thesauruses. (See Figure 5.22.)

Word Specialist Cards

One example of a dictionary-thinking activity is to have students create Be a Word Specialist! cards (see Figure 5.21). We want children to become word specialists—they need to know, understand, and use words in their personal word banks. Cards help children become word experts and are an excellent way to use dictionaries and thesauruses (Richek, 2005). To implement the activity, you can have each child make individual word cards for the Magic 8 words, or the words can be split among a group and each group member can make a card. These cards can be displayed on the walls in the classroom or stored in student vocabulary folders or binders.

Model making a word specialist card for the class. At the top of the word card, write the target word in large print. Next, have students record an original sentence featuring the target word in the space below the line. This original sentence is important because children need to refer to it when looking up the definition in the dictionary. For the words on the Magic 8 list, I find it best to create my own sentences and write them on the board. While the children copy the sentence onto their card, you can discuss possible word meanings with them. This will give the children clues to the correct definition. When children look up the definition independently, they then have a reference sentence to compare their findings to. Have the children write the definition below the sentence and finish off the card with a quick sketch or drawing of the word's meaning.

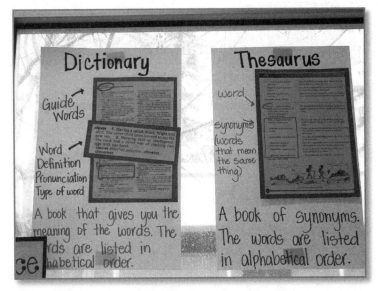

Figure 5.22: Dictionary and thesaurus guide

Important Points to Remember

Teach Vocabulary Purposefully

Know concepts that words represent.

Demonstrate a large repertoire of words readily available in your mind, and classroom, to help you read, think, speak, and write.

Teach concepts, not words.

Choose words selectively and avoid teaching lists and lists of words.

Discuss words, focus on a word and other related words, and create semantic representations of words.

Actively engage students with authentic vocabulary work.

Conveying What's Interesting About Word Parts

Teaching Points

- Learn how word parts affect word roots.

- Use word parts to decode and understand word meanings.

Prep Tip

- Prepare various charts on word parts to display in room.

Lesson Focus

I've been teaching word parts for years and I thought the goal was for children to learn what the word part meant. I was wrong. It isn't as important for children to know that *re-* means to repeat an action as it is for them to know what *re-* does to a word when I place it in front of that word (e.g., *rewrite, retype, reword*). So, put aside those rote prefix and suffix lessons! We are going to teach what the word parts *do* to a word that refines and creates meaning. After all, vocabulary instruction is about making deep meaning so our students know and understand many, many words.

There isn't just one way to teach a word-part lesson; you can approach this angle of word instruction in a variety of ways. Just keep in mind that vocabulary instruction is greater than word parts. Some state standards appear to focus heavily on word parts as vocabulary instruction, and this can be misleading. For example, the California Department of Education content standards for vocabulary instruction in fourth grade are as follows:

Vocabulary and Concept Development (CDE, 1997)

- 1.2 Apply knowledge of word origins, derivations, synonyms, antonyms, and idioms to determine the meaning of words and phrases.

- 1.3 Use knowledge of root words to determine the meaning of unknown words within a passage.

- 1.4 Know common roots and affixes derived from Greek and Latin and use this knowledge to analyze the meaning of complex words (e.g., *international*).

- 1.5 Use a thesaurus to determine related words and concepts.

- 1.6 Distinguish and interpret words with multiple meanings.

Four out of the six standards for fourth-grade vocabulary instruction are focused on word parts. This focus is *one part* of your vocabulary program, and by focusing on only one aspect of vocabulary instruction, you won't help children develop the contextual understanding they need to truly acquire words. So, by all means, teach the power of word parts, but put these parts into the context of your vocabulary program and the units of study outlined in previous chapters. While teaching word parts is important, it isn't everything. A focus on application is the best way to make studying word parts useful to children. Your lessons need to model for children how to apply the knowledge of word parts to understand unknown words and comprehend what they are reading. Studying word parts may also help children with test items that specifically test word parts. You are probably accountable for this type of testing each spring, so focus on it in moderation, but remember that accelerating children's vocabularies is your goal. Knowing and understanding many, many words is important because it affects their abilities to read and write well. Knowing word parts should be the means to an end and not be the goal itself.

Strategies for Teaching Word Parts

Effective lessons on word parts include multiple strategies:

■ Create Concept Maps

Concept maps of prefixes, suffixes, root words, homophones, pronouns, plurals, homographs, and other word parts or word types develop student understanding (Edwards, Font, Baumann, & Boland, 2004; Graves, 2004). You can teach these mini-lessons using charts that tell what a prefix or suffix is. The chart should provide lots of examples. Several ideas for charts are shown in figures 5.23 through 5.27. Figure 5.23 is a chart explaining the concept of a prefix and modeling the application of the idea using both serious and silly examples. Figures 5.24 through 5.27 are charts that demonstrate the concepts of word parts and that show children how to apply word parts to daily language use.

What a Prefix Does to a Word?

A prefix isn't a word by itself, but part of a word. It changes a word's meaning.

Re- is a prefix. It means to repeat something. Here are the words we brainstormed with re-:

redo   repeat   reshape   remake   revisit

Here are our silly words.

Reicecream: We reicecream when our ice cream falls off the cone.

Reshoe: We reshoe when mom tell us not to take off our shoes and we already did.

Recrumple: We recrumple a paper if we really think it is trash.

Figure 5.23: Students can add their own words and ideas to charts to help them remember the new concepts they're learning.

■ Use Word Webs

Webs and concept maps that link roots to new words are effective ways to help children learn about roots and information at the same time (Stahl & Nagy, 2006; Nagy, 1988). Figure 5.24 shows an example of a Semantic Map for the root *tech-*, which comes from the Greek root *techne-*, meaning "an art."

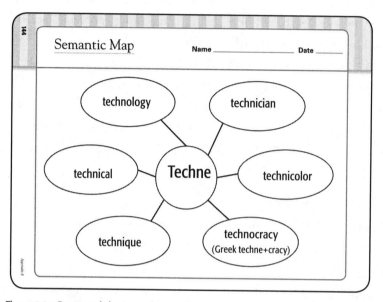

Figure 5.24: Root-word chart sample

■ Brainstorm

Nonsense words with the prefixes and suffixes

Brainstorming nonsense words and silly examples is fun (see Figure 5.23) and brings giggles to a serious subject. Most important, creating nonsense words or silly examples helps children apply learning in a unique way so they will better remember a word's meaning (Blachowicz & Fisher, 2004).

Sentences with words that have prefixes and suffixes

Writing sentences and cloze sentences (in a cloze sentence, a word is missing) together helps children learn new words and distinguish between incorrect choices (Edwards, Font, Baumann, & Boland, 2004). For example, a cloze sentence, like the one below, can be listed on charts and displayed or written on transparencies to make the discussion of word choice visual.

The reporter _____ his newspaper article many times.
Choices: *rewinds, regroups, rewrites*

Figure 5.25: Charts that focus on word parts, suffixes, and function

Figure 5.26: Charts focusing on plurals, abbreviations, and other word functions

Focus On Teaching

Your focus is important when teaching prefixes and suffixes, so you must take care in choosing the right words to teach. There are too many words and not enough time. Researchers have tallied the number of times that words containing prefixes and suffixes appear in schoolbooks and textbooks. They found that only 20 prefixes account for 97 percent of most words with prefixes that appear in school texts (Stahl, 1999). Of these prefixes, *un-* accounted for 26 percent of the words, *re-* for 14 percent, *in-*, *im-*, *il-*, and *ir-* (meaning not) accounted for 11 percent and *dis-* accounted for 7 percent (White, Sowell, & Yanagihara, 1989). Researchers found similar results with suffixes. White, Sowell, and Yanagihara found that 20 suffixes account for a large percentage of most words with suffixes in school texts. The most common were the noun endings (*-s, -es*), the verb endings (*-ed, -ing, -en*) and the adjective endings (*-er, -est*) (Stahl, 1999).

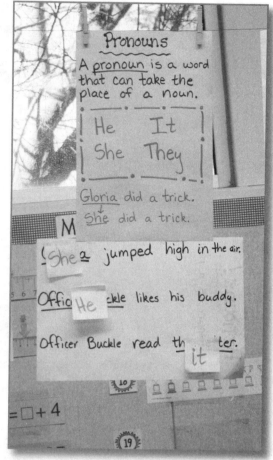

Figure 5.27: Charts that focus on pronouns

Since the goal is to teach word parts to help children get to meaning, it makes sense to focus on the word parts that occur most frequently in print. When children understand which letter patterns make a prefix or suffix, they will have an easier time of seeing the root word. This ability helps children become more fluent readers, as they can focus on word chunks, an excellent decoding strategy.

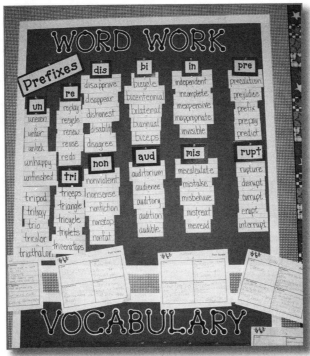

Displaying word parts on a well-organized bulletin board draws
student attention to the concepts taught in mini-lessons.

Important Points to Remember

Focus Children on Learning Just-Right Words

Throwing big words at children isn't effective.

Target words within their zone of proximal development.

Words for instruction should not be rare, or too common, they should be "just right."

Develop just-right words.

CHAPTER 6

Content Studies

How to Teach Vocabulary Using Your Social Studies and Science Textbooks

Vocabulary development in science and social studies isn't about words; it's about knowledge. Well, actually . . . it's about the kids remembering the knowledge. This isn't easy with all kids, and there have been many times I've finished a lesson and wondered how much of the information the children were able to take in. The expansive information in the social studies and science books isn't always accessible or engaging. Having a lot of information wedged into a page or chapter is very challenging for struggling readers. I often have to read, and reread, then reread again to think of ways to make the information interesting to the array of students I work with. Vocabulary development in science and social studies is about getting kids to *connect* with information so they will develop knowledge and remember words and concepts. Connection to information . . . *that* is what vocabulary instruction in the content areas is all about. Three caveats appear over and over again in research and resources that guide our teaching and show us how to help children connect to information (Beck, McKeown, & Kucan, 2002, 2003; Gutherie & Wigfield, 2000; among others):

- Be choosy about the words you teach.

- Be innovative in your approach.

- Tie rigorous reading, writing, and discussion to the content.

As you are well aware, connecting kids to facts and information is easier said than done. Perhaps this is because we are expected by curriculum guides to give the children so much to learn!

The sixth-grade science textbook used at my school weighs four pounds and is one and a half inches thick. Obviously, there are a lot of words inside of this hefty volume. The book has 21 chapters and 725 pages, and the writing is dense. The front matter lists the California standards the book addresses: seven main areas with five to seven content standards listed under each area, totaling thirty-six standards. There is a lot of information in this book to teach.

The fifth-grade book is similarly taxing. This volume is smaller and it uses a larger font and more white space per page. The larger font and white space are helpful for the struggling student as there isn't as much to comprehend on each page. But while these features help the reader, there is still an overwhelming amount of information to teach in each unit. Page B2 lists 11 words as a vocabulary preview for the first chapter in the unit B, and Chapter 2 lists 8 words as a preview. In total, this one unit recommends teaching 48 words. These recommended words include *troposphere, hurricane, forecast,* and *corona,* all of which fall into Beck, McKeown, and Kucan's (2002) Tier Three category. These 48 words recommended for direct instruction don't include other words children should have acquired in previous science studies, like *temperate, barometer, cirrus.* Recall that Tier Three words are connected directly to specific content areas and aren't considered classic academic vocabulary words (which are broader words seen in multiple genres, or what Beck, Kucan and McKeown call Tier Two words), so it is important how you define which words are worthy of direct instruction during your science and social studies lessons. Considering that you probably only have a precious 30 minutes for content instruction, you don't want to spend too much time directly teaching the words. However, you can powerfully fold the acquisition of new terms into the acquisition of new knowledge.

Be Choosy

Up until this point, the units of study have guided your students in developing word consciousness, learning word strategies, and digging deeply into the meaning of academic vocabulary words. While you don't want to move away from teaching the academic (or Tier Two) words during your Fab Fifteen, you may be feeling that the same old routine produces doldrums. Content area words are fun and provide tidbits of interesting facts and information that pique student interest; adding content words into your Fab Fifteen off and on throughout the year spices up vocabulary instruction. But add these cautiously, as the research clearly points out that the vocabulary that accelerates students' success in school consists of words seen across genres and content areas.

Remember that the Fab Fifteen is a time when you dig deep into word meanings and the concepts they represent. Content area words are different. Students need to be exposed to many words to deepen their knowledge base, but they simply won't learn every word from science or social studies to the same degree. They will be familiar with some words, others they will know, and many others they could probably explain or teach to their friends. The importance of being choosy in selecting words from content areas to teach cannot be overstated. You can't teach every word; therefore, it is important to help children hang onto the words and concepts you deem most important. I recommend teaching content area words in addition to the words you teach during your Fab Fifteen. You can teach these content words while reading the science or social studies materials.

Be Innovative

You cannot teach all the words laid out by the publisher for each unit. If you have 12 words for your current lesson in social studies, and another 12 from your science lesson, when you add in the 8 you are focusing on during your Fab Fifteen word list, you are attempting 32 words in one week. That is too many words. Research shows that it is possible to focus on 8–12 words per week with direct instruction (Beck, McKeown, & Kucan, 2002; Marzano, 2004). Research shows that academic words that sweep across genres and settings are the most important to teach directly in your Fab Fifteen, but you may be less sure about which words to teach during content time.

Keep the focus narrow by zeroing in on knowledge development. When teaching content units that offer expansive amounts of information, focus on powerful words that will enable students to better understand the chapter material. It is like looking at a landscape. You can change the view of the information from the 20,000-foot view to the 2-inch view. What I mean is that instead of pointing out that your current science unit on Earth's water has 48 words to learn and spans 142 pages, start by telling the class they will learn about the water cycle and words pertaining to the water cycle (a fifth-grade science standard in California), including *precipitation, ground water, condensation,* and *humidity.* This is the 2-inch view. Teach the words the students need to know to "get" the few pages you are focusing on. Chunk the material into shorter pieces. During this 2-inch view, "chunk" or look for connections among concepts that tie many of the content words together. In other words, examine words and connections and help children become familiar with terms. Don't teach generative word use (*I know the word well, can define it, and use it in my writing*) but familiarity (*I've heard the word and generally know what it means*).

Stahl and Fairbanks (1986) found a strong correlation, an effect size of .97, in their research between direct vocabulary instruction and words that students encountered when reading. This clearly points out that preteaching words students will read during content studies makes a difference. Focus content vocabulary instruction through the use of these strategies:

- Preteach key terms—but be choosy about which words you teach.

- Teach the key words before you read aloud, or have students read independently.

- Use innovative strategies, like Semantic Maps, to preteach words.

Accelerating Content Word Learning

The words are in bold, the chapter is long, and the print is small. You have squeezed 30 minutes out of your demanding teaching schedule for your fourth-grade social studies lesson. You open the book. The class follows. You begin to read. The class follows. You stop and ask a few questions to make sure the group is following along with you. And that is when it happens . . . those kids who always "get it" have their hands in the air, wiggling and shaking them just to make sure you notice they are ready to participate in the discussion. And the others . . . well, they are less engaged, to say the least. Two of them have their books up on end and are hiding behind them, three of them are staring at an all-important spot in the middle of their desks, and one is poking his partner's chair, clearly trying to distract his group, and you along with him.

> **The Vocabulary Zoom**
> Remember that content vocabulary is but one facet of your vocabulary program. Zoom in to learn the details necessary and then zoom out to apply to the content theme.

Many of the children who cross our thresholds each day struggle to learn (I'm sure this is no surprise to you); it is how we react that makes all the difference in the world. If you demonstrate a love for content areas, combined with a firm stance on the wonder of reading and writing, some children will come running with you on your journey, and the others will be pulled in the wake of the learning wave. A classroom without passion is a classroom where the achievement gap is definitely not addressed. Some get it and those that don't, don't.

You can change this. Focus on approaching content learning from the child's standpoint: is it boring or interesting? How you approach the subject can make a big difference (Perry, Turner, & Meyer, 2006). Focus on:

- Atmosphere

- Application

- Activities

Atmosphere

First, focus on the atmosphere: what does your classroom tell the kids about the content you are studying? I am always surprised by classrooms with environments that don't represent the learning going on. If you are studying rocks and minerals, this should be evident in the room; if your class is discovering how explorers sailed the seas to the new land, this should be evident in your classroom (de Jong & Pieters, 2006; Schraw, 2006). If you cannot devote a lot of wall space to the exploration of information, then devote a board. It is that important.

While posting vocabulary from your current unit is important, it is even better when the vocabulary is tied to facts. You can display group posters showing students' latest science investigation, a timeline of a period in history, or "Did you know . . ." facts. All of these graphics should use the important vocabulary from the current content unit and reinforce it as students' eyes gaze around the room (Nesbit & Hadwin, 2006). If precise teaching is important, then the learning environment is *everything*. It supports the children through example.

Application

How are you organizing the discussions about the content your children are learning? Do you read the chapter, lecture, expect the children to take notes and study, and then test them? The best teaching strategies involve all of the students engaging with the work. All students need a chance to think about the subject, interact with the material, and then answer questions. It is important to move away from one student's asking and responding to *all* students' asking and responding (Feldman, 2005; Schraw, 2006). By engaging all students in the work, all students have to use the vocabulary words in conversation, or in their explanations of their thinking. The students who sit back and let the eager students answer everything are not flexing their thinking muscles and are most at risk for not knowing and understanding the subject matter.

Activities

▪ Try cooperative learning structures that get all of your students involved and thinking. These activities are the means to an end: they get kids involved with the information. The point isn't to incorporate group activities or group grades into your schedule; the point is to use group activities so that students can learn the information and then be personally responsible for knowing new information and expanding their vocabularies.

Tie Rigorous Reading, Writing, and Discussion to Content

Cognitively challenging talk is the best way to ensure students are learning the content area vocabulary. First, you have to find the time for social studies and science. *I know it is difficult.* With current mandates for three to three and a half hours per day of instruction devoted to language arts, there seems little time for anything but a hurried math lesson, but remember that when children build knowledge, they have more schema to access when reading; therefore, they become better readers. Remember too that as children move beyond elementary school, the rigor of content courses and of tests like the SAT demands that students have a rich knowledge base. Hirsch (2006) states that the best way to prepare for the standardized testing our students face now and beyond elementary school is by ensuring they know lots of information about the world.

So, talk about important content in your classroom: Focus your reading block on themes from social studies, use these themes during read-aloud, and encourage English learners to talk about these themes during language workshop (Akhavan, 2006). Use supplementary leveled texts during Sustained Independent Reading so that children have the opportunity to spend time reading about the subject areas you are focused on during content time. Make it count.

Don't let kids off the hook when it comes to discussing content ideas. As mentioned earlier, with a few simple steps you can get all your students involved in the discussion of information rather than the few who always answer. Begin by restructuring how students discuss the information you read to them during content time. Move toward integrated projects in which the content your students learn during social studies and science becomes fodder for feature articles or reports during writing workshop. Assign projects that infuse history or science into the language arts block.

I highly recommend infusing your classroom with supplementary leveled texts. These texts come in an array of subjects and reading levels and are a gold mine for helping students to independently study an area in depth, take notes for a report, or prepare detailed notes for a project.

Transactional Instruction and Elaborations

Once, when I was collaborating with a colleague, and focused on having the children learn vocabulary in their content area, I found myself surrounded by a small group of students, each one wanting to check in with me and reinforce their thinking. They needed reassurance, as did the dozen or more back at their desks who were distracted, or trying to look busy, but clearly unengaged. I needed a change. I realized that even with my good intentions, I was focused on students learning the vocabulary from me, and not from one another. I was dismayed that despite my intention and efforts to create a collaborative culture, where the kids participate in the learning, I had managed to set up a transmissive lesson where the one right answer was elusive and probably going to come from me. I had to change my stance and get the kids involved. They were the ones who had to remember the words.

Moving to a transactional stance meant looking at the assignment from a different angle. When children transact with information, texts, and content, they are questioning the text, synthesizing information, and creating new viewpoints. During transactional instruction, the teacher is involved in searching for answers with them, rather than in having the one right answer.

To foster transactional instruction, I changed my focus. Instead of having students fill out their own vocabulary journals by copying from the board, I had them work in groups, deciding the best way to explain a word or group of words. Then I had the entire class take notes in their journals when the students presented their Be a Word Specialist! cards, or Semantic Maps. I required that students make their presentations multidimensional and include a linguistic component and a nonlinguistic component. Nonlinguistic components consist of mental images, pictures, or diagrams (Blachowicz & Fisher, 2000; Marzano, 2004). My goal was to increase the number of times children encountered a word and concept in a meaningful way. By having the children teach the words to one another, they truly had to know the words and present them with interest to their classmates. You can ease into this teaching in the following ways. Have students:

- State an opinion in a small group and then share with the whole class

- Create group posters showing sequences or timelines

- Create word cards and clue cards and then explain the thinking behind the clue card design

- Create fact charts about history, science, or math facts

- Use group word cards (like key words) by having each child make a card for the vocabulary ring and store it in the community basket

- Record information in content area journals

Elaborations can also be extensive, integrated projects. Cary Stolepestad, a fourth-grade teacher in California's Central Valley, has her students create an integrated project in order to apply their learning about the California gold rush. She doesn't require that they learn every tidbit about the gold rush, but that they learn how the time period deeply affected the people. Each student takes on the persona of an immigrant or California resident, researches the history of the ethnic group, and then creates a character based on library research, the Internet, and in-classroom resources. Each child in her class creates a history board relating a selected ethnic group to research on the cause and effects of the population explosion during the California gold rush. Then each child creates a fictionalized journal about their persona's life and trials. The picture below (Figure 6.1) is a history board by one student in Cary's classroom. By integrating history, language arts, statistics, and writing, Cary successfully focuses on the three caveats of word learning: Be choosy about the words you teach; be innovative in your approach; and tie rigorous reading, writing, and discussion to the content.

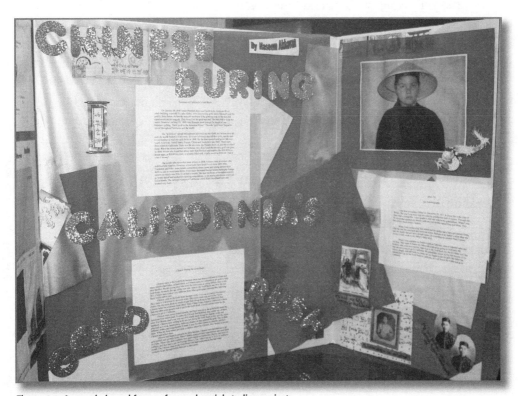

Figure 6.1: A sample board from a focused social studies project

Vocabulary Lessons That Promote Content Word Learning

The vocabulary lessons presented in this chapter are not designed as a unit of study but as an array of choices for teaching content area vocabulary. While I have concentrated on what you can do in social studies and science, some of the lesson ideas can be used for teaching math as well. These are lessons to infuse your content teaching with the direct vocabulary instruction that can make a difference for students who pretend they "get it" but breeze past the big words or say, "I don't remember," when you hold a class meeting to check what they know about your latest content study. These lessons offer respite from the "in one ear and out the other" phenomenon that occurs when children don't connect to learning.

The lessons that follow, like the lessons in previous chapters, can make a tremendous difference for children if you strike a balance between time, tension, and topic.

■ Time—Focus; keep the mini-lesson brief.

■ Tension—Avoid complacency in the children; when the lessons are relevant, they will engage with you and the work.

■ Topic—Focus on the two-inch view and then pull out to the broad view. This way you won't drown in teaching too many concepts or words, just those that are most powerful in order for the children to understand the theme of the work—for instance: how photosynthesis helps plants, or why the Revolutionary War paved the way for the civil rights movement.

Teaching Vocabulary in the Content Areas

Lesson 1: Creating Word Clue Cards

Teaching Point: Create word clues that connect to the content words from a current social studies or science unit.

Lesson 2: Using Semantic Maps to Teach Concepts

Teaching Point: Words are categorized in Semantic Maps as they relate to a topic.

Lesson 3: Learning From Attributes Chart

Teaching Point: Create a feature chart after delving deeper into a content unit.

Lesson 4: Learning From Definition Word Maps

Teaching Point: Connect other terms to the word by having students describe the word in adjectives.

Lesson 5: Dazzling Descriptive Words

Teaching Point: Elicit phrases that describe a feature, item, or thing.

Lesson 6: Teaching Children to Assess Their Word Knowledge

Teaching Point: Using a self-analysis sheet helps children tune into words they need to learn.

Figure 6.2

LESSON 1

Creating Word Clue Cards

Teaching Points

■ Students create word clues that connect to the content words from a current social studies or science unit.

■ Student ownership of the word clues makes the words and the activity relevant.

■ By exchanging cards with another student, or group, children can try to outsmart their friends through engaging and witty word clues.

Prep Tips

■ Prepare different types of cards for students to record information.

■ Use 3" x 5" index cards, or cards cut in fancy shapes. See below for an example.

Lesson Focus

Reinforce how the children's memories operate by letting them create clues for words. The clues, acting almost as definitions, give the student who designs them a way to think creatively about a word, and it gives other students who work with the cards the opportunity to practice

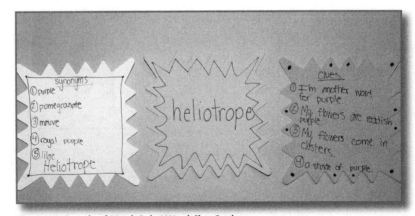

Figure 6.3: Sample of Match Point! Word Clue Cards

with definitions and attributes of content area words. Letting students create the clues helps make the words relevant to the children, and when words and word meanings are relevant, children have a better chance of remembering them (Jensen, 1998).

Give students two 3 x 5 cards for each word. On one card have them write a word, and on the other card have them write the clues describing what the word means. Consider this example (see Figure 6.3) for the word *heliotrope:* What is a plant that has purple flowers and loves the sun?

LESSON 2

Using Semantic Maps to Teach Concepts

Teaching Points

- Words are categorized as they relate to a topic.

- Children focus on how words connect to one another.

- Relationships between words are visually represented.

- Categories can include class, properties, examples, and elements.

Prep Tips

- Have construction paper or chart paper available in a variety of sizes.

- Have markers available for students to use when drawing a Semantic Map similar to that in Figure 6.4 or 6.5.

- Three Semantic Maps are available in Appendix B (pages 144–146).

Semantic Map 2   Name _____ Date _____

Lesson Focus

Semantic mapping is a one-size-fits-all activity. It works well when teaching vocabulary in any content area, including math and music. Young children can enhance Semantic Maps with pictures and drawings, and older students can connect ideas to nonlinguistic structures. What is great about semantic mapping is that children define the relationships between the words and concepts through talk and thinking (Wolfe, 2001). This reinforces their ownership of the connections and the maps. The focus isn't on the relationships, but on learning the words. The Semantic Maps on the next page offer two examples, but these maps don't require a specific setup or design; the circles just need to connect in some way as the concepts flow around and together.

   In this lesson, adapted from Stahl and Nagy (2006), I like to begin by brainstorming all the words students know about a topic, which I collect in one long list. *Water Music: Poems for Children* by Jane Yolen (1995) offers a perfect example of this kind of list. This beautiful book begins with an annotated definition of water; then Yolen's beautiful poems are paired with pictures of water. This text is an engaging supplement to the classroom library and serves as an excellent example for this activity. You will want to teach this lesson using your content area textbooks; however, beautiful nonfiction books provide a respite and enrich your textbook journey. Some of the terms I would choose from Yolen's book include: *water, frozen, chemical compound, essential, substance, sleet, tears, plant cells, gaseous, liquid.*

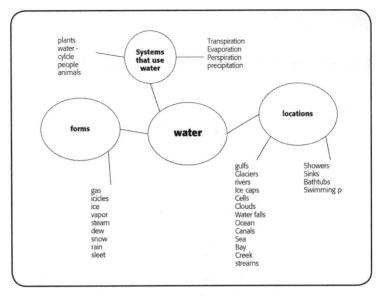

Figure 6.4: Semantic Maps help students understand how words connect to ideas, information, and facts.

After the brainstormed list is finished, I talk with the children and together we come up with three or four categories that describe the words on the list. (See Figure 6.4.) Using colored markers, I circle words in different colors that match the categories the children suggested. I group similar words together by circling them in the same color.

Then we are off to the reading. It is always important to revisit the map after reading the book to add new learning and discuss the connections again. We might add new words or draw lines between words to connect them. Sometimes we have to refine our thinking.

Research shows that Semantic Maps increase vocabulary growth for children who struggle to read, and that by focusing on the connections between the words and concepts, children can improve their comprehension of what they read (Baker, Simmons, & Kame'enui, 2005). Figure 6.5 is an example of a Semantic Map using pictures, for use with young children or English learners.

Figure 6.5: A Semantic Map using pictures

Learning From Attribute Charts

Teaching Points

▪ Use words students are familiar with.

▪ Get the students to do the talking; have them explain why a word meets or doesn't meet a criterion.

▪ Add new words to the chart after delving deeper into the content unit.

Prep Tip

▪ Prepare a Feature Array on a large piece of paper (see Figure 6.6 as an example), or use a transparency of a Feature Array (page 147, Appendix B).

Feature Array

Name _____ Date _____

Items/things	Spine	Feathers	Wings	Rays	Feet	Eyes
caterpillar					X	eye spot only
bird	X	X	X		X	X
housefly			X		X	X
cicadas		X			X	X

Figure 6.6

Lesson Focus

After you have drenched your students in enthusiasm for the social studies or science unit you are teaching, they will have enough knowledge to analyze words at a deeper level. A Feature Array is a chart where children compare a set of words with a set of criteria (Paynter et al., 2005; Stahl & Nagy, 2006). It works best to do a Feature Array Chart after the children have some familiarity with the words, because you want them to *think*. My goal for the children is to flex those thinking muscles, as I already know the answers. I want the answers to come from the group. When completing a chart, I facilitate the discussion with questions such as these:

- "What do you think . . . ?"

- "Does this item share the same properties as this other one? Why or why not?"

- "Why do you disagree? Tell me what you know about this word in relation to the criteria at the top of the chart."

1. Down the left-hand side of the chart, write words you are focusing on.

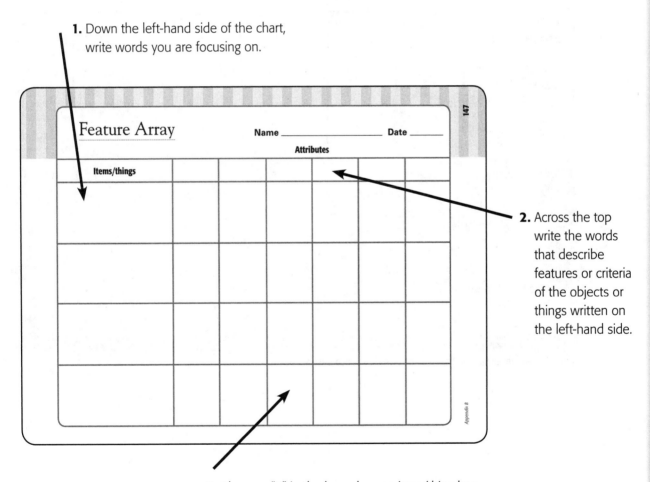

2. Across the top write the words that describe features or criteria of the objects or things written on the left-hand side.

3. Place an "X" in the box when an item/thing has the features of the attribute.

For the Feature Array, I usually choose words that are a bit more concrete and words I consider essential to the unit we are learning. Across the top of the grid I write the criteria against which we will compare the set of words. See the example on page 116.

Then we compare each word through discussion against each criterion listed across the top. If a word meets the criterion, I make an X in the corresponding box. Figure 6.7 is an example of a Feature Array from a second-grade science lesson.

Bugs	Insect?	Food they eat?	Parts of the Body?	Enemies?	Color?	Life Cycle?
Butterfly Know-It-Alls Butterflies! by Darlene Freeman						
Worm Bug Books: Worms by Jill Bailey						
Spider Spiders Up Close by Robin Birch						

Figure 6.7: An Attributes Chart for a second-grade science lesson

Learning from Definition Word Maps

Teaching Points

- Teach words that represent broad ideas.

- Have students think of examples of the word.

- Connect other terms to the word by having students describe the word in adjectives.

Prep Tips

- Make photocopies of a Definition Word Map from Appendix B (page 150).

- Review the science chapter you will be teaching for key terms to define.

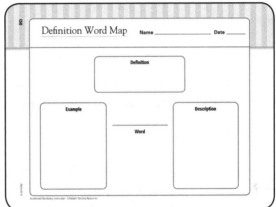

Lesson Focus

There will be words that cover broad ideas that you want students to know well and be able to define. Sometimes these far-reaching words are the ideas holding together topic units in your textbooks (Schwartz & Raphael, 1985). Such content words are holding tanks for the ideas in the chapter, and students have to learn them.

It is best to begin a Definition Word Map after reading the introductory pages to your content unit. You will want to use key terms from your science text. For this example lesson, I have used the book *Lead* by Salvatore Tocci (2005). See figure 6.9 for an example of a Definition Word Map for the term *lead*.

At the beginning of the lesson, I reviewed the features of the book with the children and then I paused and asked the children, "So what is lead anyway?" What the children said to explain the

Figure 6.8: Front cover and a page from the book *Lead*

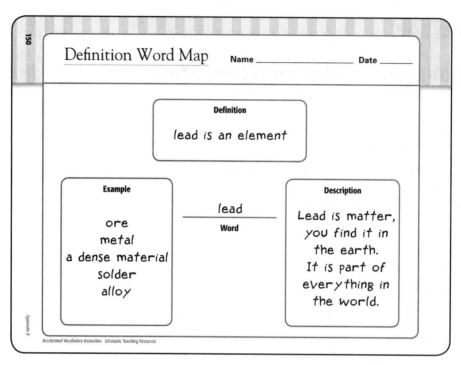

Figure 6.9: Investigating the concept of lead with a word map

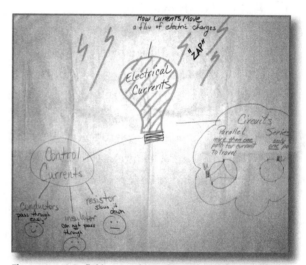

Figure 6.10: A Definition Word Map from a lesson on electricity

idea is what I wrote in the box above the word on the map. Before I continued reading, I asked the children if they could think of any examples of other ways to describe lead. I wrote the examples they told me in the box on the left side of the word.

I finished reading the book. I wanted the children to make connections between the main word and descriptive words, so I asked the children to describe lead in words, like bullets, or jots. Notice the information presented to children in the book *Lead*. The key information from the book, part of it found on this sample page, is recorded in the definition Word Map. Another example of the concept of a definition map is above (Figure 6.10). This is a sample map that a teacher made to accompany vocabulary from a science unit.

Dazzling Descriptive Words

Teaching Points

- Elicit phrases that describe a feature from a current content unit.

- List the phrases around a main-idea word.

- Don't settle for plain language; have students describe words with imaginative phrases.

Prep Tips

- Prepare large charts by using chart-stand paper or large pieces of butcher paper. (See Figure 6.11 for an example.)

- Draw a circle in the middle of the paper and write the target word.

- Do not draw the lines stemming from the circle until brainstorming words with the class.

Figure 6.11: Words and phrases describe the main word.

Lesson Focus

In Cary Stolepestad's fourth-grade classroom, she adds features of interest to her room, such as concept walls, vocabulary charts, book rings filled with persuasive student-written essays about what books to read and why, science stations, and a full library. She creates a fabulous milieu for children to soak in daily. But she doesn't stop there. Cary also encourages children to think about the concepts and the words they know about their current social studies units. She calls these semantic maps "Dazzling Descriptive Words." On the dazzling words charts, Cary focuses the children on a main idea. She writes this in the center circle, and then she maps out their thinking in stems and bubbles off the main word. But Cary doesn't settle for one-word answers; instead, she seeks phrases. For example, when creating a chart of geographic features, her students called the plains "the flat, grass-covered sheets of land." Figure 6.11 is an example of one of Cary's charts.

Teaching Children to Assess Their Word Knowledge

Teaching Points

- When children read nonfiction they need to be aware of important words they don't understand.

- Using a self-analysis sheet helps children tune into words they need to learn. (See ideas for assessment in Chapter 2.)

- The children set personal goals by picking words they want to learn and words that help them understand their reading.

- Students define the terms in their own words and draw a picture to remember the word.

- Teach the "Think It, Ink It" strategy; if they have a question about a word, or a wondering, or a confusion, they *ink it* in their journals or on a self-assessment sheet (see Figure 6.12) in order to remember to examine the word further.

Prep Tips

- Copy self-assessment sheets for each student (page 153, Appendix B).

- Choose words from an article (see Figure 6.13) or textbook that children may need help learning.

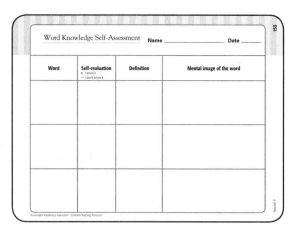

Lesson Focus

Children should be reading lots and lots of nonfiction text. It helps them gather broad knowledge about the world in general and gives them the opportunity to learn their favorite subjects in depth. There are many trade books and small leveled texts that provide great supplementary material in content areas. I love these supplementary texts because children can gather in-depth knowledge about core subject areas for report writing, general knowledge-building, and, of course, for word learning.

But the best way to use the plethora of nonfiction reading available to children is to help them focus on a few words in their reading. When children self-assess, they naturally set learning goals for themselves and usually feel more motivated to learn. Focusing on their own ideas is more empowering than focusing on the teacher's ideas for word learning.

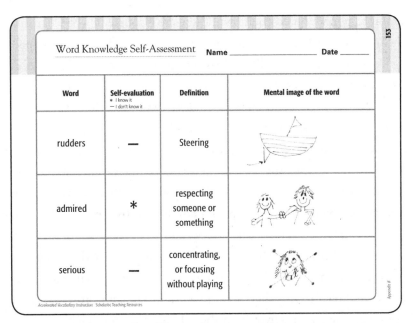

Figure 6.12: Self-assessment sheet for learning unknown words

Figure 6.13: A *Scholastic News* article helps children become independent word learners.

When children read nonfiction on their own, there are a couple of word-learning strategies that can help them. Take a look at the *Scholastic News* article in Figure 6.13. The feature article, entitled "Daring Dogs," is on Newfoundland dogs acting as lifeguards (Scholastic, 2006). The article is chock-full of words that can trip up a student's comprehension. Two words are in boldface, *rudders* and *admired*. You can increase student comprehension of the material read and ensure that children remember some vocabulary words by having them identify the words that are in boldface in the text. Remind them to return to the boldface words to help them if they don't understand what they are reading. By taking this step, you are encouraging them to become independent word learners. In addition, have children identify other words in the article that give them a bit of trouble. Some problem words for children in this feature article might include *serious, nature, webbed, rudderlike,* and *rescue*. They can record these words and assess their understanding of the words from the context, carefully applying what they have learned thus far in the text or from accompanying graphics. The children can write their unknown word on a self-assessment sheet and refer to this sheet later to learn unknown words. Figure 6.12 is one student's self-assessment sheet for the words on the "Daring Dogs" article.

One word-learning strategy that works well for children is to have them stop at the end of each paragraph and ask themselves:

- Do I understand what I am reading?

- Are there any words I can't pronounce?

- Are there any words I am unsure of?

- What do I think this word means?

If the children find words they don't know, it is important to have them write the words down. "Think It, Ink It" is an important routine. You can also expand "Think It, Ink It" and have children write down interesting words they know and understand that help them comprehend what they are reading. You might introduce this idea by saying, "I can never remember everything that is important, so if I think something is important, I write it down immediately. If I think it, I ink it. I want you do this while you are reading the *Scholastic News* article. Write down any word in your self-assessment sheet that you are unfamiliar with and want to learn."

Important Points to Remember

Remember the
Levels of Knowing Words

Association Level:
(think of connecting ideas or associating ideas)

"I am familiar with the word; I remember seeing or hearing it before."

Comprehension Level:
(think of comprehending an idea or information)

"I know the word and understand what it means."

Generation Level:
(think of generating ideas or information)

"I know the word well; I can use it in my conversations or in my writing."

CHAPTER 7

The Current Research

Why Good Instruction Is Central to Students' Word Acquisition and Future Success

Accelerating word learning is difficult. Accelerating learning means that we have to be purposeful, focused, and intent. Children need us to help them learn. They need us to focus each and every day to provide them with the material they need to know so that they can have the world at their feet. It is up to us.

Because it is up to us, we have to take time to plan well. When you plan time to teach vocabulary, focus on the information research reveals about vocabulary instruction. This book has examined some ways that you might do that. This book has presented units of study based on findings from various reading researchers who have focused their studies on vocabulary acquisition processes and methodology. As this book has pointed out in lessons and classroom examples, vocabulary development does not need to reduce a classroom focused on authentic, meaningful, and integrated instruction to traditional rote learning. In fact, traditional vocabulary instruction like memorizing definitions and copying sentences are incongruent with the current research-based understanding of effective reading and vocabulary instruction.

The Complexity of Word Knowledge

William Nagy and Judith Scott wrote a chapter on vocabulary processes in the third volume of *Handbook of Reading Research*, entitled "Vocabulary Processes" (2000). This work reminds readers of the complexity and depth of vocabulary acquisition. Defining what it means to know a word is complex and multidimensional. Five aspects of this complexity have been recognized by vocabulary researchers over time:

- Incrementality—We know words by degree, it is not all or nothing.

- Multidimensionality—Knowing words consists of different types of knowledge.

- Polysemy—Words have multiple meanings.

- Interrelatedness—Our knowledge of words is connected to our knowledge of other words.

- Heterogeneity—What it means to know a word differs, depending on the kind of word.

Different Ways of Knowing Words

We don't know all words to the same degree. Some words we own. We know them so well we can use them in any context, generate them in writing and conversation as needed, and completely understand all possible uses of the word. Knowing a word in this manner is called the "generation" level of word knowledge (Marzano, 2004; Stahl & Nagy, 2006; Stahl, 1999). In essence, the word can be generated or retrieved from memory and used correctly. We do this all the time with high-frequency words, but what gives our vocabulary breadth and depth is having generative knowledge of words that don't appear as often in writing or conversation.

The other two levels of word knowledge are "association" and "comprehension." When we know a word at the association level, we might not understand what the word means, but we can make correct associations about the word (Marzano, 2004). When we know a word at the comprehension level, we know the commonly accepted meaning of the word, but we don't own the word or use it in our repertoire (Marzano, 2004; Stahl, 1999).

The research behind knowing words is multifaceted and includes knowing the grammatical contexts and connotations of words (Beck, McKeown, & Kucan, 2002). While these dimensions are important, this book focuses on the three levels of word knowledge offered by Stahl: association, comprehension, and generation. Nagy and Scott (2000) demonstrate that we might know the definition of a word but still be confused about the appropriate use of it, and they discuss how words are interrelated. So, in order to think of word-learning applications in our elementary classrooms, we need to realize that we know words at various levels and to various degrees. In addition, our knowledge of words prepares us to make associations to new words when we encounter them (Beck et al., 2002; Nagy & Scott, 2000).

Three Important Principles of Vocabulary Development

Stephen Stahl's work provides important and bountiful information on vocabulary acquisition and on effective methodologies and activities. Three important principles that stem from his research are as follows (Stahl, 1999; Dougherty & Stahl, 2005):

- Provide definitional and contextual information about a word's meaning.

- Provide multiple exposures to meaningful information about words.

- Actively involve children in learning word meanings.

Authentic and Purposeful Word Learning

When integrated into content and motivating curriculum, word learning is authentic and purposeful. Stahl suggests that a child has to hear and collect experiences about a word about 12 times before that word is acquired (Stahl, 1999). While a child can fast-map a word or concept upon hearing it once or twice, it takes at least 12 experiences with a word to acquire it and own it. Children need to use words to move their learning from Fast Mapping to deep, powerful learning. When they use words meaningfully, or for academic conversations, writing, and writing about reading, they will have purpose and utility for new words.

Fast Mapping Word Meaning

Susan Carey's work studying how young children learn words revealed a difference between Fast Mapping a word's meaning and extending mapping of a word's meaning. Carey (1978) described Fast Mapping as taking place with one or two encounters with a word. She noted that this was enough exposure for a child to develop a rudimentary mental lexicon that represents some of a word's syntactic and semantic features. Fast Mapping is important as it affects the rate of vocabulary growth in children. If a child has encounters with many words and multiple encounters with a word, a child will build a deep understanding of a word's meaning and use.

Fast Mapping as an Instructional Tool

Fast Mapping is a learning structure in which children with few experiences with a new word begin to form an understanding of the word. In Fast Mapping, children don't learn all the concepts about a word, but some syntactic and semantic features of the word and a simple understanding of the word are remembered (Carey, 1978; Nagy & Scott, 2000). Fast Mapping is the connection the brain makes when first learning a word. We don't *own* the word when our brains have mapped it quickly, but we are on our way to truly knowing it. This is the beginning step. If students can learn eight to ten words a day, they can fast-map additional words in their brains and do so without noticing.

Fast Mapping is the key to accelerating children's vocabulary learning. Carey's research shows that if children are able to remember the specific linguistic or nonlinguistic context in which a word was first heard or seen, then the child can build a more extensive understanding of its meaning and its nuances. This occurs best through nonlinguistic examples, including hearing people use and explain a word, seeing objects and pictures, and tying remembered information to the picture, object, or experience.

Carey's research shows that some features of a word's meaning are remembered early, and others acquired later. This is why Fast Mapping can give us a quick understanding of a word (as in "I've seen it or heard it, but I can't explain it"), and how repeated exposure to a word increases the brain map that enables us to understand and own a word.

Schema Theory and Vocabulary Learning

Alina Reznitskaya and Richard Anderson point out in "The Argument Schema and Learning to Reason" (2001) that the idea of schemas as a way to represent and process information has been part of cognitive psychology for many years. They define schemas as skeleton knowledge structures. Schemas influence vocabulary development.

Schemas serve a variety of functions affecting learning, comprehension, and remembering. Schemas also influence the development and construction of meaning by integrating new learning into existing knowledge structures. Reznitskaya and Anderson posit that social interaction through collaborative reasoning helps children develop the skills of argument discourse. Argument discourse encourages children to make inferences and discuss their ideas, by developing an argument stance with text and words, which state and support their claims. Schemas are important in learning because they direct our brain's resources, including:

- Perception

- Comprehension

- Learning

- Remembering

Schemas do all of the following:

- Influence the construction of meaning

- Integrate new learning into existing structures in our brain (connections)

- Provide a niche for information that aids learning

- Enable inferencing; schemas help us make predictions about incoming information and guide interpretation of the incoming information

- Guide the process of remembering as they reinterpret stored memory

The Importance of Schemas

Schemas are an important organizational unit in our memory. Schemas are organized information about an area, or domain, for which we have knowledge. They provide a niche, or spot in our brains, for the assimilation of new information. Information that fits into existing slots is easily learned with little effort. Schemas enable us to construct meaning from what we already know and expect from past experiences and learning. Schraw (2006) concluded that schemas are essential to learning for several reasons. Schemas are:

- Integrating—We can organize large amounts of information into an existing body of knowledge.

- Structured—Information is encoded and retrieved in an organized and efficient manner.

- Activated—We use our schemas to make predictions, form hypotheses, and interpret information.

- Dynamic—We can change our schemas when new information is encountered.

Tapping Prior Knowledge Means Tapping Into Schemas

Thinking of schemas as information storage houses brings new meaning to "tapping prior knowledge." At the beginning of a lesson we engage children and wake up their brains. We want them to remember things they know that connect to the new information we are going to teach. By connecting new information to their existing schema, students can learn the new information we present to them. So we can accelerate word learning by connecting words to the concepts students already know, and we can help them develop conceptual understanding through a large amount of reading and content study.

Vocabulary Instruction Practices

The National Reading Panel

The National Reading Panel results (NICHD, 2000 pp. 4–27) attempted to report the relationships between vocabulary and reading comprehension. The report states that reading comprehension comprises two skills: word knowledge or vocabulary and reasoning. Vocabulary is strongly related to reading comprehension.

According to the National Reading Panel, implications for vocabulary instruction include the following:

- Vocabulary should be taught both directly and indirectly.

- Repetition and multiple exposures to vocabulary items are important.

- Learning in rich contexts is valuable for vocabulary learning.

- Vocabulary tasks should be restructured when necessary.

- Vocabulary learning should entail active engagement in learning tasks.

- Computer technology can be used to help teach vocabulary.

- Vocabulary can be acquired through incidental learning.

- How vocabulary is assessed and evaluated can have differential effects on instruction.

- Dependence on a single vocabulary instruction method will not result in optimal learning.

Good Practice Equals Learning

When we provide connected learning, we are accelerating the rate at which children learn and know new words. We have to focus on how we teach so that we help our students understand that expanding their vocabularies is important. By providing both explicit and implicit opportunities to learn words, we can help children move beyond the short, quick phrases they use for daily friend-to-friend communication and learn new discourses. In sum, we teach them how words are used in school and in life and how words connect us to the world.

CHAPTER 8

Against the Odds

Succeeding With Vocabulary Instruction

It was a beautiful June day and I was about to meet with a group of students to talk about words: words they knew, words that made them think, beautiful words that flowed with emotion, and words that opened doors. I pulled open the door to Melissa Jones's summer literacy program and her students were spread out about the room. They had positioned themselves to read; most were strategically near the fan that whirred quietly in the background to ward off the summer heat. Some fanned themselves to deal with the stuffy, humid room, while most were lying as still as possible, moving only their fingers to turn pages. I settled on the floor with Jesse to listen to him read. He was midway through *Nate the Great and the Monster Mess* (Sharmat, 1999). "I love Nate the Great!" he said.

"Really? Can you read some of it to me? Just begin wherever you left off."

"Anywhere on the page?"

"Yes, anywhere. Just begin."

And he did. Jesse read rapid fire. He bounced through words he didn't know, dropped a few word endings, and changed a few words to have the sentences remain semantically and syntactically correct. His reading was fluid and effortless. His mistakes, or miscues, were small and didn't affect his fluency. I began to wonder why he was in this special summer program. He had entered fourth grade, and his teacher had recommended him for summer school. I suspected that perhaps he didn't comprehend everything he read.

"Wow, Jesse, you can read this book out loud well! Is it too easy? Maybe it isn't a just-right book?"

Jesse's eyes clouded over. "I like *Nate the Great*." I wasn't surprised by this reaction. What child wants to switch from a book he loves? But I felt I needed to dig deeper.

"Oh, of course, and I am glad about that. I was just wondering if you tried something just a bit more challenging when I meet with you, then I can help you with strategies to figure out new words."

"I can still read *Nate the Great?*"

"Yes."

"Are you sure?"

"Yes! But go ahead and tell me about the story first. What has happened so far?"

To my surprise, Jesse bounded off into a detailed explanation of what had occurred so far in the story. He described the action and the characters. But through this quick and fast account of his reading, I noticed that Jesse talked in general terms, never describing the character or the action in specific words. He talked *around* the text.

"So what does Nate the Great do?"

"He looks for stuff when people lose things. Like that boy, he lost his cat."

"Oh, so Nate the Great, he finds things for people?"

"Yeah, he looks for stuff. I've seen people like him on TV."

"Do those people have a name, like a title?"

"I dunno. I guess . . . . Can I read now?"

As Jesse picked up his book and stretched back on the floor, I saw the problem. Jesse didn't know the words to describe what was happening in the story. He knew the plot and the character but was limited in his ability to generate words to describe the action. It was at that moment I knew why he was in this summer program: he needed to develop his vocabulary. He understood the action in this early chapter book, but he lacked the expressive vocabulary to describe his understanding.

Honestly, this came as no surprise to me. I snapped my notebook shut and looked around the room. The room was filled with children from different backgrounds, all working on reading, savoring the moment, really, reading, licking a finger from time to time, and turning a page. I wished I could see inside their heads. I wondered how many of them truly understood what they were reading, or if they could tell me about their reading, using language that was both accurate and rich. I looked back at Jesse, deep into his book. I wondered if I could teach Jesse the word *detective* before he finished that *Nate the Great* title.

Melissa Jones, Jesse's summer literacy teacher, picked her way around the children spread out across the classroom. With her anecdotal notebook in her hand, her face was set with determination.

"It's really interesting," she said, flipping the pages. "Most of the students need help with vocabulary. I noticed while listening to them read. They are fluent but they can't retell using words from the story. *And* when they do get stuck on a word, most of them pause, figure it out, but have no idea what the word means."

"Do you think they are inexperienced with talking about their books?" I asked.

"Well, no, I've watched them do this in class throughout the school year, and I know that their teachers taught words and word meanings last year. It's like the learning didn't stick. I don't think the children really learned the words."

"Maybe." I smiled while glancing at the information in her notebook.

"Or, maybe," Melissa said, "there are many words to teach and many contexts to read them in, and we just have to keep going."

"It's true, you know," I added. "Children often learn words, learn ways to think, talk, and express themselves at a specific text level, but when they move to the next grade, and try a harder book, well, it's like they have to learn the next set of skills and abilities to talk about their books and their writing. Now that Jesse is in fourth grade, I expect more of his responses. I want him to be more articulate about how he talks about books and information. I guess it is the next step; we just have to keep going."

Melissa nodded and looked down at her notes and then at the students in her class. "I think that's it; we just have to keep going!"

The Stamina to Improve Children's Learning

Success takes driving focus, relentless passion, and patience balanced with rigor. I have seen just this mix in many, many classrooms. And in those classrooms children learn and thrive. Something else happens in these programs as well: test scores improve. Vocabulary instruction shouldn't be only about test scores—it should be about children and their success. However, test scores are a reality that we face, so we must pay attention.

When you focus your instruction and capture every minute of the day and tie it up with purposeful instruction based on current grade-level standards, your children will succeed. When you have relentless passion for all children to learn, and focus your energy on creating an incredibly rich and supportive classroom, your children will succeed. And when you have patience, but not too much patience, with children who work at rigorous assignments designed to close the achievement gap, your children will succeed. The key is not giving up, and not watering down your curriculum.

I know this firsthand. I work as principal at Pinedale Elementary School in a poverty-impacted neighborhood in California. When we focused on effective literacy instruction, including reading, writing, and vocabulary, our spring scores on the California Standards Test rose steadily. After two years of focus and infusing our classrooms with words, print, and authentic reading and writing through workshops, we met expected growth targets laid out by the federal No Child Left Behind law.

We can all be successful with the children filling our classrooms. Perhaps after a year of vocabulary instruction you will find your children are using words in ways you never dreamed of. Perhaps your colleagues at the next grade level will be thrilled with how her students use words in their discussions and writing. Perhaps you will find the energy in words that I have found working with teachers across the country as we discussed the beauty of our classrooms dripping with words, the power that our favorite words have in our instruction, and the way we feel when those words that educate us and connect us to our children roll off our tongue. Just perhaps.

Suggested Read-Aloud Titles

Title	Author	Publisher	Focus Words
Stand Tall, Molly Lou Melon	Patty Lovell	G. P. Putnam's Sons, 2001	believe, proud, foolish, mind
Wallace's Lists	Barbara Bottner and Gerald Kruglik	Katherine Tegen Books, 2004	lists, nervous, adventure
Hey, Little Ant	Phillip and Hannah Hoose	Tricycle Press, 1998	squish, feel, beneath
Mice and Beans	Pam Muñoz Ryan	Scholastic Press, 2001	Numerous Spanish words, all listed in a glossary at the back of the book
Snog the Frog	Tony Bonning	Barron's, 2004	Onomatopoeic words
Three Cheers for Catherine the Great	Cari Best	Sunburst Books, 1999	presents; perfect; various descriptive phrases like "toes tapped out"
How the Stars Fell into the Sky: A Navajo Legend	Jerrie Oughton	Houghton Mifflin, 1992	legend, first woman, mosaic, laws
If You Listen	Charlotte Zolotow	Running Press, 2002	lonely, listen, distance, inside
Bob	Tracy Campbell Pearson	Farrar, Straus, and Giroux, 2002	Onomatopoeic words; crow, terrified, amazed
What's the Magic Word?	Kelly DiPucchio	HarperCollins, 2005	whoosed, kerplunk, magic word
The Raft	Jim La Marche	HarperCollins, 2000	river rat, carving, ancient, preened, nuzzle, wildness
Scarecrow	Cynthia Rylant	Voyager Books, 1998	borrowed, gentleness, witness, housed

Accelerated Vocabulary Instruction © 2007 by Nancy Akhavan • Scholastic Teaching Resources

Suggested Read-Aloud Titles

Title	Author	Publisher	Focus Words
Won't You Be My Kissaroo?	Joanne Ryder	Gulliver Books, 2004	Phrases to describe kisses: "breakfast kiss", "playful kiss"
Old Turtle and the Broken Truth	Douglas Wood	Scholastic Press, 2003	truth, examined, broken, mysterious, understood, suffering, beauty
A Packet of Seeds	Deborah Hopkinson	Greenwillow Books, 2004	sorrow, journey, prairie, cabin, spirits, gladden, sass, hatchet, abed
The Name Jar	Yangsook Choi	Dell Dragonfly Books, 2001	strange, nervous, excited, characters, curious, identity, grace
Beatrice Doesn't Want To	Laura Numeroff	Candlewick Press, 2004	comfy, all of a sudden, bored, driving me crazy, ignored
Love Is a Family	Roma Downey	Scholastic, 2002	real, weirdest, stepdads, stepmoms, half
The Little Scarecrow Boy	Margaret Wise Brown	Joanna Cotler Books, 1998	scarecrow, fierce, scare, rattle, ragged
Apple Fractions	Jerry Pallota	Cartwheel Books, 2002	Various mathematical terms: fraction, divide, separate, equal parts, whole, numerator, denominator, medium, largest, smallest, improper fraction
The Paperboy	Dav Pilkey	Scholastic, 1996	softly, asleep, snapping, loaded down, by heart, sounds of morning

Accelerated Vocabulary Instruction © 2007 by Nancy Akhavan • Scholastic Teaching Resources

Suggested Read-Aloud Titles

Title	Author	Publisher	Focus Words
Tackylocks and the Three Bears	Helen Lester	Houghton Mifflin, 2002	happening, perform, waddled, exhausted, odd
When the Moon Is High	Alice Schertle	HarperCollins, 2003	Poetic phrases including: pocket peeking, hide and seeking, wild wind riding, getting prowly
Little Raccoon's Big Question	Miriam Schlein	Greenwillow, 2004	poke, proud, huddle, stroked, whatever
The Wolves in the Walls	Neil Gaiman	HarperCollins, 2003	hustling, crackling, crumpling, squabbling, schemes, ignorance, dreadful, treasured possessions
When Marian Sang	Pam Muñoz Ryan	Scholastic Press, 2002	remarkable gift, contralto, colored, prejudice, professional, segregated, humiliations, dignity
Saturdays and Teacakes	Lester L. Laminack	Peachtree Publishers, 2004	pooling, directly, dew-wet, reckon, ingredients
Luke's Way of Looking	Nadia Wheatley	Kane/Miller, 2001	portrait, differently, rage, imagination, ballistic, sightseeing, empowerment
Crickwing	Janell Cannon	Voyager Books, 2000	creatures, sculptures, cowering, dodged, darted, massive, crevice, exoskeleton, groggy, punier, twerp

Suggested Read-Aloud Titles

Title	Author	Publisher	Focus Words
My Mama Had a Dancing Heart	Libba Moore Gray	Orchard Books, 1995	Various literary phrases including: Tip-tapping, song-singing, finger-snapping, hold-on-tight, leg-lifting, sing-swelling
A Bad Case of Stripes	David Shannon	Blue Sky Press, 1998	Fretting, disaster, distraction, contagious, embarrassed, scientific, bizarre, lima beans, cured
Dear Mrs. LaRue: Letters From Obedience School	Mark Teague	Scholastic Press, 2002	obedience, resident, misconceptions, escape, lummox, nightmare, appreciated, bluffing, misunderstood
Sweet Dream Pie	Audrey Wood and Mark Teague	Blue Sky Press, 1998	draped, enormous, blame, blissful, conservatory, snuggle, sweep
Ruby in Her Own Time	Jonathon Emmett	Scholastic Press, 2003	howling, shook, nothing, precious, soared, beyond, everywhere, high, distance
My Favorite Things (According to Alberta)	Emily Jenkins	Anne Schwartz Books, 2004	particular, tastes, convinced, bitter, adores, appreciate

Accelerated Vocabulary Instruction © 2007 by Nancy Akhavan • Scholastic Teaching Resources

Unit of Study

Name _____ Date _____

Monday	Tuesday	Wednesday	Thursday	Friday

Use this reproducible to create a transparency for the activity that begins on page 34.

Two-Category Sort

Name _____ Date _____

Category:

Category:

Use this reproducible to create a transparency for the activity that begins on page 85.

Accelerated Vocabulary Instruction © 2007 by Nancy Akhavan • Scholastic Teaching Resources

Four-Category Sort

Name _____ Date _____

Category:

Category:

Category:

Category:

Accelerated Vocabulary Instruction © 2007 by Nancy Akhavan • Scholastic Teaching Resources

Use this reproducible to create a transparency for the activity that begins on page 84, or use the transparency provided in the envelope at the back of this book.

Four-Square Word Map

Name _____ Date _____

1. Target Word	2. Example
Dictionary Definition:	
3. My Definition	4. Non-Example

Use this reproducible to create a transparency for the activity that begins on page 82, or use the transparency provided in the envelope at the back of this book.

Appendix B

Accelerated Vocabulary Instruction © 2007 by Nancy Akhavan • Scholastic Teaching Resources

Just-Right Word List

Name _____

Date _____

Use this reproducible to create a transparency for the activity that begins on page 91.

Just-Right Word List Record Sheet

Name _____ Date _____

Word	Picture	My Definition

Accelerated Vocabulary Instruction © 2007 by Nancy Akhavan • Scholastic Teaching Resources

Appendix B

Name _____

Magic 8!

1.

2.

3.

4.

5.

6.

7.

8.

Name _____

Magic 8!

1.

2.

3.

4.

5.

6.

7.

8.

Use this reproducible to create a transparency for the activity that begins on page 77.

Semantic Map

Use this reproducible to create a transparency for the activity that begins on pages 64 and 112.

Appendix B

Name _____

Date _____

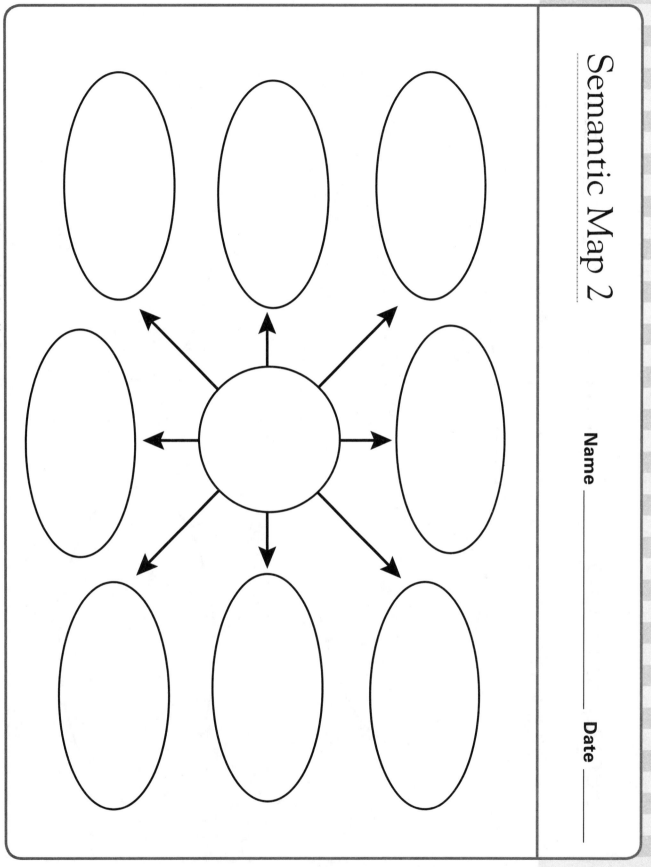

Use this reproducible to create a transparency for the activity that begins on page 112.

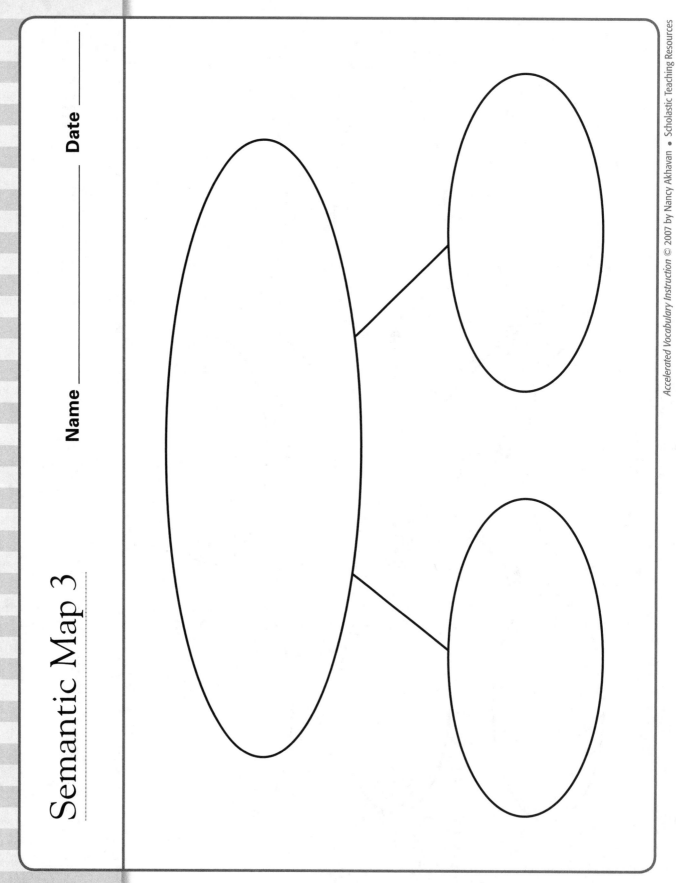

Use this reproducible to create a transparency for the activity that begins on page 112.

Accelerated Vocabulary Instruction © 2007 by Nancy Akhavan • Scholastic Teaching Resources

Feature Array

Name _____ Date _____

Items/Things				Attributes		

Use this reproducible to create a transparency for the activity that begins on page 114, or use the transparency provided in the envelope at the back of this book.

Be a Word Specialist! Card

Name _____ Date _____

Word	
Original Sentence:	**Picture**
Definition:	

Use this reproducible to create a transparency for the activity that begins on page 93, or use the transparency provided in the envelope at the back of this book.

Accelerated Vocabulary Instruction © 2007 by Nancy Akhavan • Scholastic Teaching Resources

Appendix B

Word Map

Name _____ **Date** _____

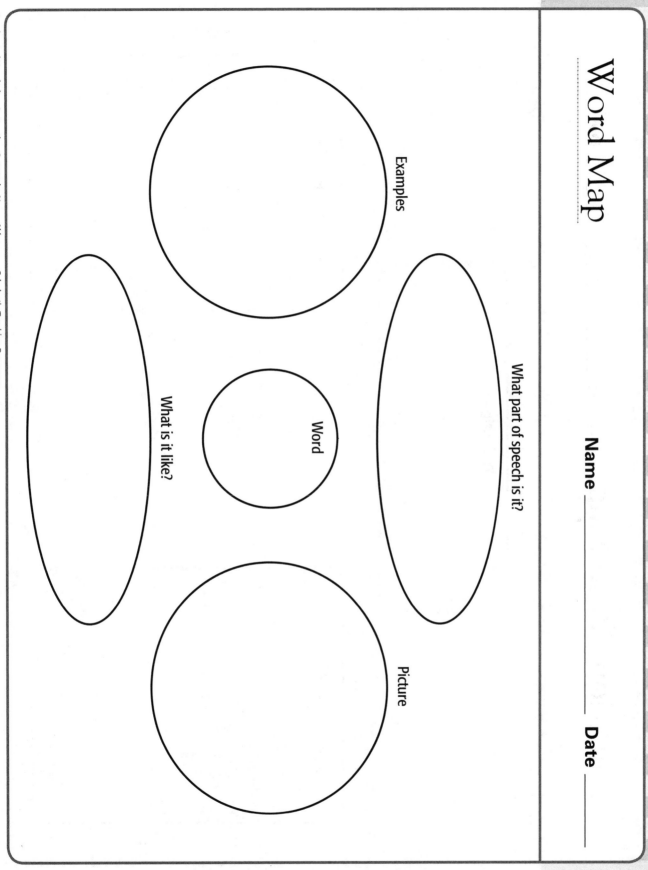

Examples

What part of speech is it?

What is it like?

Word

Picture

Use this reproducible to create a transparency for the activity that begins on page 81, or use the transparency provided in the envelope at the back of this book.

Definition Word Map

Name _____

Definition

Description

Word

Example

Use this reproducible to create a transparency for the activity that begins on page 117, or use the transparency provided in the envelope at the back of this book.

Accelerated Vocabulary Instruction © 2007 by Nancy Akhavan • Scholastic Teaching Resources

Name _____ Date _____

Word Picture Activity

Directions: Write the target word in the first box. Sketch the picture you have in your mind when thinking of that word. Next, Look/Think/Write. Look at your picture, think of other words that describe your picture, write those words in the box. These words will help you remember the meaning of the target word.

Target Word	
My Word Sketch	
Look / Think / Write	

Use this reproducible to create a transparency for the activity that begins on page 47, or use the transparency provided in the envelope at the back of this book.

Word Card

Name _____ Date _____

Word	Definition in my own words

Use this reproducible to create a transparency for the activity that begins on page 35.

Appendix B

Accelerated Vocabulary Instruction © 2007 by Nancy Akhavan • Scholastic Teaching Resources

Word Knowledge Self-Assessment

Name _____   Date _____

Word	Self-evaluation ∗ I know it — I don't know it	Definition	Mental image of the word

Use this reproducible to create a transparency for the activity that begins on page 120,
or use the transparency provided in the envelope at the back of this book.

Name _____

Date _____

Brainstorm words below the line that begin with the letter in the box.

It's a Word Thing!

Write a letter in the box.

Use this reproducible to create a transparency for the activity that begins on page 46, or use the transparency provided in the envelope at the back of this book.

Accelerated Vocabulary Instruction © 2007 by Nancy Akhavan • Scholastic Teaching Resources

Appendix B

References:
Children's Literature

Cane, M. (1994). Snow toward evening. In B. Rogasky (Ed.), *Winter poems* (p. 16). New York: Scholastic.

Child, L. (2001). *Beware of the storybook wolves.* New York: Arthur A. Levine.

DePalma, M. N. (2005). *A grand old tree.* New York: Arthur A. Levine.

Holt, K. W. (2002). *My Louisiana Sky.* New York: Hyperion.

Jenkins, E. (2004). *Daffodil.* New York: Farrar, Straus and Giroux.

Lipp, F. (2001). *The caged birds of Phnom Penh.* New York: Holiday House.

Lu, C. (2006). Cool inventions: Ultimate water ride. *National Geographic Kids. 362,* p. 23.

Norlander, B. (2006). And they're off! *Science World, 63* (11), 22–23.

Paulsen, G. (1987). *Hatchet.* New York: Bradbury Press. reprint: 1999 New York: Simon & Schuster.

Polacco, P. (1998). *My rotten redheaded older brother.* New York: Aladdin.

Robinson, F. (1999). *A dinosaur named Sue: The find of the century.* New York: Scholastic.

Daring Dogs (2006). *Scholastic News, 62* (25), 2.

Ryan, P. M. (1999). *Amelia and Eleanor go for a ride.* New York: Scholastic.

Ryan, P. M. (2001). *Esperanza rising.* New York: Scholastic.

Rylant, C. (2004). *Long night moon.* New York: Simon & Schuster.

Rylant, C. (1998). *Tulip sees America.* New York: Blue Sky Press.

Sachar, L. (2004). *Sideways stories from wayside school.* New York: Harper Trophy.

Sharmat, M. (1999). *Nate the Great and the Monster Mess.* New York: Delacourt Books for Young Readers.

Sheth, K. (2004). *Blue jasmine.* New York: Hyperion Books for Children.

Spinelli, E. (2001). *Sophie's masterpiece: A spider's tale.* New York: Simon & Schuster.

Tocci, S. (2006). *Lead.* New York: Scholastic.

Yolen, J. (1995). *Water music: Poems for children.* Honesdale, PA: Boyds Mills Press.

References:

Professional Resources

Akhavan, N. (2004). *How to align literacy instruction, assessment, and standards: And achieve results you never dreamed possible.* Portsmouth, NH: Heinemann.

Akhavan, N. (2006). *Help! My kids don't all speak English: How to set up a language workshop in your linguistically diverse classroom.* Portsmouth, NH: Heinemann.

Allington, R. (2005). *What really matters for struggling readers: Designing research-based programs* (2nd ed.). Boston: Allyn & Bacon.

Baker, S., Simmons, D., & Kame'enui, E. (2005). Vocabulary acquisition: Synthesis of the research. Retrieved April 14, 2006, from http://idea.uoregon.edu/%7Encite/documents/techrep/tech13.html.

Bear, D. R., & Helman, L. (2003). Word study for vocabulary development in the early stages of literacy learning: Ecological perspectives and learning English. In J. F. Baumann & E. J. Kame'enui (Eds.), *Vocabulary instruction: Research to practice* (pp. 139–158). New York: Guilford.

Bear, D. R., Invernizzi, M., Templeton, S. R., & Johnston, F. (2003). *Words their way* (3rd ed.). New York: Prentice Hall.

Beck, I., McKeown, M. G., & Kucan, L. (2002). *Bringing words to life: Robust vocabulary instruction.* New York: Guilford.

Beck, I., McKeown, M. G., & Kucan, L. (2003). Taking delight in words: Using oral language to build young children's vocabularies. *American Educator, 27,* 36–41.

Biemiller, A. (1999). *Language and reading success.* Brookline, MA: Brookline Books.

Blachowicz, C., & Fisher, P. (1996). *Teaching vocabulary in all classrooms.* Columbus, OH: Allyn & Bacon/Merrill.

Blachowicz, C., & Fisher, P. (2000). Vocabulary instruction. In M. L. Kamil, P. B. Mosenthal, P. D. Pearson, & R. Barr (Eds.), *Handbook of reading research* (Vol. 3) (pp. 503–524). Mahwah, NJ: Lawrence Erlbaum Associates.

Blachowicz, C., & Fisher, P. (2004). Keep the fun in fundamental: Encouraging word awareness and incidental word learning in the classroom through word play. In J. F. Baumann, & E. J. Kame'enui, (Eds.) *Vocabulary instruction: Research to practice* (pp. 218–238). New York: Guilford.

California Department of Education. English language arts standards, grade four. Retrieved July 19, 2006, from http://www.cde.ca.gov/be/st/ss/enggrade4.asp

Calkins, L. (2001). *The art of teaching reading.* Boston: Allyn & Bacon.

Cambourne, B. (2002). Holistic, integrated approaches to reading and language arts instruction: The constructivist framework of an instructional theory. In A. E. Farstrup & S. J. Samuels (Eds.), *What research has to say about reading instruction* (pp. 25–47). Newark, DE: International Reading Association.

Carey, S. (1978). The child as a word learner. In M. Halle, J. Brennan, & G. A. Miller (Eds.), *Linguistic theory and psychological reality* (pp. 265–293). Cambridge, UK: Cambridge University Press.

Carlo, M. S., August, D., McLaughlin, B., Snow, C. E., Dressler, C., Lippman, D. N., et al. (2004). Closing the gap: Addressing the vocabulary needs of English-language learners in bilingual and mainstream classrooms. *Reading Research Quarterly, 39*(2), 188–215.

Coyne, M. D., Simmons, D. C., & Kame'enui, E. J. (2004). Vocabulary instruction for young children at risk of experiencing reading difficulties: Teaching the word meanings during shared storybook readings. In J. F. Baumann & E. J. Kame'enui (Eds.), *Vocabulary instruction: Research to practice* (pp. 41–58). New York: Guilford.

Daane, M. C., Campbell, J. R., Grigg, W. S., Goodman, M. J., & Oranje, A. (2005). Fourth-grade students reading aloud: NAEP 2002 special study of oral reading (NCES 2006-469). U.S. Department of Education, Institute of Education Sciences, National Center for Education Statistics. Washington, DC: Government Printing Office.

De Jong, T., & Pieters, J. (2006). The design of powerful learning environments. In P. A. Alexander & P. H. Winne (Eds.), *Handbook of educational psychology* (pp. 739–754). Mahwah, NJ: Lawrence Erlbaum Associates.

Dougherty Stahl, K. A. (2005). Improving the asphalt of reading instruction: A tribute to the work of Steven A. Stahl. *The Reading Teacher, 59*(2), 184–192.

Edwards, E. C., Font, G., Baumann, J. F., & Boland, E. (2004). Unlocking word meanings: Strategies and guidelines for teaching morphemic and contextual analysis. In J. F. Baumann & E. J. Kame'enui (Eds.), *Vocabulary instruction: Research to practice* (pp. 159–178). New York: Guilford.

Eeds, M, & Cockrum, W. (1985). Teaching word meanings by expanding schemata vs. dictionary work vs. reading in context. *Journal of Reading, 28*(6), 492–497.

Feldman, K. (2006). "Narrowing the Language Gap: Active Engagement." Clovis Quality Improvement Seminars. Clovis, CA.

Fountas, I. C., & Pinnell, G. S. (1996). *Guided reading: Good first teaching for all children.* Portsmouth, NH: Heinemann.

Goldsberry, S. T. (2004). *The writer's book of wisdom: 101 rules for mastering your craft.* Cincinnati, OH: Writer's Digest Books.

Graves, M. F. (2004). Teaching prefixes: As good as it gets? In J. F. Baumann & E. J. Kame'enui (Eds.), *Vocabulary instruction: Research to practice.* (pp. 81–99). New York: Guilford.

Graves, M. F., & Watts-Taffe, S. M. (2002). The place of word consciousness in a research-based vocabulary program. In A. E. Farstrup & S. J. Samuels (Eds.), *What research has to say about reading instruction* (pp. 140–165). Newark, DE: International Reading Association.

Gutherie, J. T., & Wigfield, A. (2000). Engagement and motivation in reading. In M. L. Kamil, P. B. Mosenthal, P. D. Pearson, & R. Barr (Eds.), *Handbook of reading research* (Vol. 3) (pp. 403–424). Mahwah, NJ: Lawrence Erlbaum Associates

Hart, B., & Risley, T. R. (1995). *Meaningful differences in the everyday experiences of young American children.* Baltimore, MD: Brookes Publishing.

Hart, B., & Risley, T. R. (2003, Spring). The early catastrophe: The 30 million word gap by age 3. *American Educator.* Retrieved September 16, 2006, from http://www.aft.org/pubs-reports/american_educator/spring2003/catastrophe.html

Hayes, D. P., & Ahrens, M. G. (1988). Vocabulary simplification for children: A special case of "motherese"? *Journal of Child Language, 15*(2), 170–175.

Hirsch, E. D., Jr. (2003). Reading comprehension requires knowledge—of words and the world. *American Educator, 27*(1), 10–24.

Hirsch, E. D., Jr. (2006). *The knowledge deficit: Closing the shocking education gap for American children.* Boston, MA: Houghton Mifflin.

Hoyt, L. (2002). *Make it real: Strategies for success with informal texts.* Portsmouth, NH: Heinemann.

Jensen, E. (1998). *Teaching with the brain in mind.* Alexandria, VA: Association for Supervision and Curriculum Development.

Jensen, E. (2000). *Brain-based learning: The new science of teaching and training.* (Rev. ed.) San Diego, CA: The Brain Store.

Kamil, M. L., Mosenthal, P. B., Pearson P. D., & Barr, R. (Eds.). (2000). *Handbook of reading research* (Vol. 3). Mahwah, New Jersey: Lawrence Erlbaum.

Livingston, A., & Wirt, J. (2005). *The condition of education 2005 in brief* (NCES 2005-095). U.S. Department of Education, National Center for Education Statistics. Washington, DC: US Government Printing Office.

Marzano, R. J. (2004). The developing vision of vocabulary instruction. In J. F. Baumann & E. J. Kame'enui (Eds.), *Vocabulary instruction: Research to practice* (pp. 100–117). New York: Guilford.

Marzano, R. J., Pickering, D., & Pollack, J. E. (2001). *Classroom instruction that works: Research-based strategies for increasing student achievement.* Alexandria, VA: Association for Supervision and Curriculum Development.

Mayer, R. E., & Wittrock, M. C. (2006). Problem solving. In P. A. Alexander & P. H. Winne (Eds.), *Handbook of educational psychology* (pp. 287–304). Mahwah, NJ: Lawrence Erlbaum Associates.

McKeown, M. G., & Beck, E. L. (2004). Direct and rich vocabulary instruction. In J. F. Baumann & E. J. Kame'enui (Eds.), *Vocabulary instruction: Research to practice* (pp. 13–27). New York: Guilford.

Nagy, W. E. (1988). *Teaching vocabulary to improve reading comprehension.* Newark, DE: International Reading Association.

Nagy, W. E., & Anderson, R. C. (1984). How many words are there in printed school English? *Reading Research Quarterly, 19*(304), 330.

Nagy, W. E., & Scott, J. S. (2000). Vocabulary processes. In M. L. Kamil, P. B. Mosenthal, P. D. Pearson, & R. Barr (Eds.), *Handbook of reading research* (Vol. 3) (pp. 269–284). Mahwah, NJ: Lawrence Erlbaum Associates.

Nation, I. S. P. (2001). *Learning vocabulary in another language.* Cambridge, MA: Cambridge University Press.

National Institute of Child Health and Human Development (NICHD). (2000). Report of the national reading panel: Teaching children to read. Reports of the subgroups. Washington, DC: National Institute for Literacy.

Nesbit, J. C., & Hadwin, A. E. (2006). Methodological issues in educational psychology. In P. A. Alexander & P. H. Winne (Eds.), *Handbook of educational psychology* (pp. 825–848). Mahwah, NJ: Lawrence Erlbaum Associates.

Neuman, S. B., & Celano, D. (2006). The knowledge gap: Implications for leveling the playing field for low-income and middle-income children. *Reading Research Quarterly 41*(2), 176–201.

Paynter, D. E., Bodrova, E., & Doty, J. K. (2005). *For the love of words: Vocabulary instruction that works.* San Francisco, CA: Jossey-Bass.

Perry, N. E., J. C. Turner, & D. K. Meyer. (2006). Classrooms as contexts for motivating learning. In P. A. Alexander & P. H. Winne (Eds.) *Handbook of educational psychology* (pp. 327–348). Mahwah, NJ: Laurence Erlbaum Associates.

Pinnell, G. S., & Fountas, I. C. (2004). *Word study lessons: Letters, words, and how they work: Grade 3.* Portsmouth, NH: Firsthand.

Pratt, H., & Pratt, N. (2004). Integrating science and literacy instruction with a common goal of learning science content. In W. E. Saul (Ed.), *Crossing borders in literacy and science instruction: Perspectives on theory and practice* (pp. 395–405). Newark, DE: International Reading Association.

Reznitskaya, A., & Anderson, R. C. (2002). The argument schema and learning to reason. In C. Block & M. Pressley (Eds.), *Comprehension instruction: Research-based best practices* (pp. 319–336) New York: Guilford.

Richek, M. A. (2005). Words are wonderful: Interactive, time-efficient strategies to teach meaning vocabulary. *The Reading Teacher 58*(5), 414–423.

Samuels, S. J. (2002). Reading fluency: Its development and assessment. In A. E. Farstrup & S. J. Samuels (Eds.), *What research has to say about reading instruction* (pp. 166–183).Newark, DE: International Reading Association.

Scarcella, R. (2003). Academic English: A conceptual framework. Linguistic Minority Research Institute, The University of California, Irvine, CA (Technical Report 2003-1).

Schwartz, R. M., & Raphael, T. E. (1985). Concept of definition: A key to improving students' vocabulary. *The Reading Teacher, 39*(2), 198–205.

Schraw, G. (2006). Knowledge structures and processes. In P. A. Alexander & P. H. Winne (Eds.), *Handbook of educational psychology* (pp. 245–264). Mahwah, NJ: Lawrence Erlbaum Associates.

Scott, J. A., & Nagy, W. E. (2004). Developing word consciousness. In J. F. Baumann & E. J. Kame'enui (Eds.), *Vocabulary instruction: Research to practice* (pp. 201–217). New York: Guilford.

Shefelbine, J. (2004). Lecture delivered October 12, 2004. California Reading Association Conference, San Jose, CA.

Short, D., & Echevarria, J. (2004). Teacher skills to support English language learners. *Educational Leadership, 62*(4), 8–13.

Stahl, S. A. (1985). To teach a word well: A framework for vocabulary instruction. *Reading World, 24*(3), 16–27.

Stahl, S. A. (1999). *Vocabulary development.* Brookline, MA: Brookline Books.

Stahl, S. A. (2003). Words are learned incrementally over multiple exposures. *American Educator 27*(1), 18–19.

Stahl, S. A., & Fairbanks, M. (1986). The effects of vocabulary instruction: A model-based meta-analysis. *Review of Educational Research, 56*(1), 72–110.

Stahl, S. A., & Nagy, W. E. (2006). *Teaching word meanings.* Mahwah, NJ: Lawrence Erlbaum Associates.

Stahl, S. A., & Stahl, K. A. (2004). Word wizards all!: Teaching word meanings in preschool and primary education. In J. F. Baumann & E. J. Kame'enui (Eds.), *Vocabulary instruction: Research to practice* (pp. 59–80). New York: Guilford.

Stanovich, K. (1986). Matthew effects in reading: some consequences of individual differences in the acquisition of literacy. *Reading Research Quarterly.* Fall 1986, p. 360–406. Volume XXI, no. 4.

Stiggins, R. (2004). New assessment beliefs for a new school mission. *Phi Delta Kappan, 86*(1), 22–27.

Suen, A. (2002). *Picture writing: A new approach to writing for kids and teens.* Cincinnati, OH: Writer's Digest Books.

Wade, S. E., & Moje, E. B. (2000). The role of text in classroom learning. In M. L. Kamil, P. B. Mosenthal, P. D. Pearson, & R. Barr (Eds.), *Handbook of reading research* (Vol. 3) (pp. 609–628). Mahwah, NJ: Lawrence Erlbaum Associates.

White, T. G., Sowell, J., & Yanagihara, A. (1989). Teaching elementary students to use word-part clues. *The Reading Teacher, 42*, 302-309.

Winn, I. J. (2004). The high cost of uncritical teaching. *Phi Delta Kappan, 85*(7), 496–497.

Wolfe, P. (2001). *Brain matters: Translating research into classroom practice.* Alexandria, VA: Association for Supervision and Curriculum Development.

158

Index